Interpreting the Bible

A Simple Introduction

Rev. James A. Fischer, C.M.

PAULIST PRESS
New York / Mahwah, N.J.

Cover design by Moe Berman.

Cover photo by Joseph Taney.

Library of Congress Cataloging-in-Publication Data

Fischer, James A.
    Interpreting the Bible : a simple introduction / by James A. Fischer.
        p.   cm.
    Includes bibliographical references.
    ISBN 0-8091-3653-8 (alk. paper)
    1. Bible—Hermeneutics. I. Title.
BS476.F57 1996
220.6'01—dc20   96-21584
                                                                    CIP

Published by Paulist Press
997 Macarthur Boulevard
Mahwah, New Jersey 07430

Printed and bound in the
United States of America

Contents

THIS BOOK IS DEDICATED TO
REV. FRANCIS BRUCE VAWTER, C.M.
1921–1986

PIONEER OF BIBLE POPULARIZATION
STUDENT, CONFRERE, FRIEND

◆　　◆

Acknowledgment:
To Amy Stevens who has been a most helpful editor of this book my thanks.
To my students who have challenged me to think.

Introduction

For years I have taught courses on the bible and taken part in discussion groups. It has always struck me that the participants have been so unimpressed at times by the opinions of "experts," supposedly including myself, and then again so perceptive of meanings which were legitimate and deeply spiritual. They had convictions within themselves—sometimes self-confusing—which were more powerful than my scholarly background. Something deeper was guiding their conclusions.

As I thought over this normal mystery of a teaching career, I began to isolate some of these informal roots of conviction. The deeper I got, the more fascinating it became. At some point I invented the expression "Resident Alien" for these undercurrents of conviction, both good and bad. The name seemed to say something to students and to a more general public. So I began to study in both my teaching and my learning what this was all about. I found not only that it was helpful (1 Tim 3:15 says that all scripture is "useful" and I think that must apply to all commentary as well) but that it revealed something most important about the reasons why we should hold on to our faith. It is not new; indeed, it is a most conventional view of what we mean by "tradition" or "the sense of the faithful." And yet this is something of a new look at an old topic which is especially meaningful for us today when so many bases of our beliefs seem to be in disarray.

The scriptural texts cited here are from the New American Bible. Endnotes are appended to each chapter which will suggest where you may find further information. Perhaps too you may find a use for them as a backup for the main text. I have tried to write in an informal way and yet I am conscious of my duty to the reader to have researched the matters I am dealing with.

I hope that you may enjoy this journey into the unknown and yet knowable as I have in writing it.

Rev. James A. Fischer, C.M.

1

The Problem

1. Understanding Classic Stories

The western novel or movie has a classic form. One day a stranger in a white hat comes riding into town. He makes friends with an oppressed rancher or farmer and has a mild romance with his pure daughter. The town, of course, is run by an unscrupulous boss and his thugs. The conflict finally comes to a crisis between the good guy and the bad guy. Something like the shoot-out at the O.K. Corral develops and the town goes on with peace and justice. In the last scene the hero is seen "riding out of town as the sun sinks slowly into the west."

We all know the story although it is not often told today in the classic form. Historians have replaced the romance with a picture of the real west. Or it has become a simple story of good guys and bad guys. But it has also lost its ability to touch us. We knew that there was a larger story behind the classic story. The story of the hero who comes from some place unknown, saves the town and then disappears into the mysterious west again speaks to us of the broader human situation which can be rescued only by some hero from out there.

Why don't we resonate to these hidden but basic stories? To be more specific, why do our interpretations of scripture seem so shallow, divergent and so ineffective in meeting contemporary needs? Today, for example, in the United States we have a severe division among our citizens over abortion. Christians are on both sides of the issue. The text for one side is: "Thou shalt not commit murder" and the interpretation stops at the law. The other Christians cite less concise texts on freedom and equal dignity and conclude that abortion is a right of the woman to decide. No amount of explaining the texts persuades the other side. Nor do our presentations seem to have much effect on the general public. Something seems to be missing. The conclusions seem to have been made before the texts were cited.

Perhaps we can learn a little bit—only a little bit—from street gangs. They seem to have little difficulty in presenting a united front which is effective. Those who examine such matters find that street gangs have created their own strong identity. They have their heroes in the stories they tell, they have a strong discipline and they are sure of their cause. The price they pay for this is too great, but it cannot be denied that their interpretation of life, however perverse, is working.

These are practical problems of interpretation. The abortion example is nearer to the immediate point since it derives largely from biblical texts. But the mythology of the street gangs is closer to the real sources of interpretation of events.

Even the experts are aware that something has gone disastrously wrong with our way of interpreting the bible and with the influence it has on society.[1] Often an appeal is made to get back to the identifying stories of our culture and religion, both the undergirding stories of myth and the continuing stories of our society. The story world does not exist simply as an entertainment. It is the world behind the world. It has its own reality even before it is connected with historical fact. The reality is that of our common humanity, our real experiences that shape lives and dictate action.

2. The Purpose of This Book

Christians and others today have a desire to find spiritual meaning for their lives. The bible is a principal source. The popularity of books of inspiration, prayers, meditations and bible discussion materials attests to it. It is a large item in the publishing business. Yet the search for authentic spirituality is skewed by factors which escape us. Scholars, who have a great influence on what is said in popular presentations, have come of late to understand that they have little entry into spiritual values which meet this need. I have no solution for this problem, but the ancient definition of theology says that theology is faith seeking understanding. Perhaps we need more understanding of how that seeking goes on. The search is inevitable, and that is what this book is about.

This book does try to look at the problem of what is behind our conclusions which we claim to derive from the bible. Why do we hold them as absolutely necessary and yet we disagree so much among ourselves? The bible is one; the history of its use is multiple, to say the least. Why do people who agree that this book is the basis of their religion come to such different conclusions?

Scholars are in no better shape. For the past hundred years or more scholars have often concentrated on that ideal called objectivity or at least rational demonstration. Unfortunately, they have seldom agreed among themselves, either on methods or especially on larger, practical conclusions. What does emerge rarely lasts for generations or centuries.[2] It waxes as the initial ideas are discussed and then wanes as it becomes overly sophisticated and loosened from its bonds to daily living. Indeed, it is sometimes the affectation of biblical scholars that they have no responsibility or very little to do with religious belief in contemporary society. They simply study the facts like any other scientists. Yet the personal element must necessarily enter in.

Nor is the matter much different in other religions. Muslims are as much divided as Christians. Jews are a marvel of divergent interpretations. Even the more recent churches, such as the Mormons, show a tendency to come to a parting of the ways over what the founding documents actually mean.

3. Interpreting Foundational Documents

All the major religions of the world have some story or document which energized them. Interpreting foundational documents, especially ancient ones, is admittedly a risky business. One must first know the language. With the bible that is not a major problem at first sight. We know Hebrew, although we are still discovering surprising corrections in our texts and in our translations. Greek is well known and still a living language although considerably changed. Yet we do not know these languages as we do our native ones. There are implications, code words, nuances, transpositions which only a native speaker picks up easily.

Were we to be able to listen to the original Christians in their street life, we might be surprised or baffled by what they were saying as they used their everyday language. Our culture is so different that we would not immediately pick up on all of their meanings.

Perhaps we do not even understand ourselves well enough as Christians to know how we are contaminating our reading of the bible from other sources. We already have interpreting codes within us from other sources than our Christian tradition. A computer can run various programs but we need to avoid becoming confused over which program we are running. We need to know more about the program or method from which we begin to act as Christian interpreters.

4. The Resident Aliens in Our House

Among the hidden interpreters who are at work within us there are those which I shall call the Resident Aliens. These interpreters are alien to both the text and the method which we think we are using. But they are resident. We cannot get rid of them. They come from the powerful ways of shaping conclusions which arise from our family, our ethnic origin, our national consciousness, our education, our stage of growth, etc. We shall need to look at this later. And yet behind it all is a commonality of a story of the human family. Jung presumed that there were primordial archetypes which account for the commonality of mythological themes and which Joseph Campbell later popularized as a monomyth under the title of *The Hero with a Thousand Faces*.[3] So we have these Resident Aliens residing in our common house.

At any rate, it is this instinctive way of reacting to a text which determines much of who we are and how we react. Every country has a national anthem. It often means very little musically or poetically to foreigners. It stirs the patriots to deep emotions and resolutions. It is the Resident Alien who gives meaning.

5. *The Final Problem*

The final problem is the one which all revealed religions with a sacred book must face. Individuals may interpret the foundational document as they will, but this does not define what the cohesive group believes. In Catholic theology we call it the *sensus fidelium*, "the sense of the faithful"; George Lindbeck called it the "classic hermeneutic," that is, "the one which the 'nuclear' Christians discover they believe in times of crisis and are willing to die for."[4]

Unfortunately, this *sensus fidelium* does not operate equally in all areas. Catholic theologians in the past have tried to devise a menu of doctrinal normativity, called theological notes, which pinpoints where on the scale of certitude various teachings and opinions lie. At the top were the professedly *de fide* absolute pronouncements of popes and councils—whether there was priority here was never quite cleared up. Then came conclusions reached on logical principles more immediately or remotely connected. Then there was the consensus of theologians. At the very end was a negative note called "offensive to pious ears." Only there did the "faithful" seem to have a voice in the *sensus fidelium*. The priority listing was devised for doctrinal matters but inevitably it slipped into moral use. In ethics no absolute decisions stood at the top precisely similar to *de fide* decisions. The decisions of officials based more or less on logic and precedent plus the consensus of theologians were the most important. Most such decisions involved the Roman curia, the bureaucracy. When Vatican II began its description of the church from the people of God, it challenged the security of the system. But it did not replace it with something else.[5]

The problem is that the *sensus fidelium* "the understanding of the faithful," is not only vague in its parameters but also in its creativity. It cannot be tied down completely once and for all. If we say that we are certain about the *sensus fidelium* in those things which the Catholic Church has defined *de fide*, we are also aware that there are variant interpretations of what the defined doctrine actually said. Meanwhile the interpretation of the people of God as they apply the gospel to contemporary needs constantly readapts itself as it preserves the basic faith. As all agree, this is a matter of creatively preserving the tradition, not of doing what we think best and then taking an opinion poll. The *sensus fidelium* embraces all, everywhere and throughout the history of the church.

This is not a uniquely Catholic approach. The early Lutheran standpoint was that the church was marked by "authentic preaching" and the sacraments. The sacraments were generally reduced by common understanding to baptism and eucharist, with the other traditional ones given some lesser level of reality. "Authentic preaching" was never clearly defined, although in the sociology of the movement it came to mean what the group approved.

The final problem is to define the *sensus fidelium* in a legitimate and operative way. I have no intention of trying to do so. My goal is much more modest. I want only to investigate something of what does go into the *sensus fidelium*. Perhaps then we can recognize something more of the common understanding of the present faith of the Catholic Church and find some small bit of common understanding for our contemporary needs.

6. A Road Map of This Book

I shall begin with contemporary stories and needs. We understand them more easily. Investigating the universe with radio-telescope technology is real and operating today. Our fascination with it is focused on the possibility, however remote, that we may hear something from someone out there. In the second chapter I shall look at how the bible is aimed at the same thing, and sometimes the techniques are astonishingly similar.

In the third chapter I want to consider how religious seers

have always tried to authenticate the message they were delivering. The fourth chapter deals with that underlying myth of the need for salvation which groups all over the world have always found imperative. Perhaps after this in Chapter 5 we can discover something about why the scholars and we ourselves have had such a difficult time of dealing with all those Resident Aliens.

As we come to understand both the problems and the need for something solid into which we can sink our teeth, we shall survey how Christians have always been about the work of interpreting their basic story. Chapter 6 begins with Paul as the first writing interpreter, and then Chapter 7 moves on to the people of God within the Roman Catholic Church as they have interpreted the scriptures through the ages. Chapter 8 will investigate how the Resident Aliens affect us personally for good or bad. The next chapter shall attempt to sum up all of this and define partially how Catholic Christians have recognized the "nuclear" Christians among themselves. The conclusion is clear: at the end is only faith; it is not provable but is endures as the only way we can enter into the mysteries of our lives.

ENDNOTES

1. Richard John Neuhaus, *Biblical Interpretation in Crisis: The Ratzinger Conference on Bible and Church* (Grand Rapids: Eerdmans, 1989), brought out this point forcibly if not clearly. The introductory lecture by Cardinal Ratzinger, "Biblical Interpretation in Crisis: On the Question of the Foundations and Approaches of Exegesis Today" (24–49), centered on the failure of contemporary historical exegesis to find an entrance into the "God factor" in its quest for facts. The ensuing discussion of the group in the final chapter (102–190) by Paul T. Stallsworth entitled "The Story of an Encounter" centered mainly on this theme. Raymond Brown's defense of the historical-critical method was basically that it had helped us to understand how the biblical texts developed and what they meant in the era of their production. Brown also concluded that his personal experience of lecturing indicated that audiences still found this useful for their personal lives. However, this does not address the question of how they made

this transfer. George Lindbeck's "classic hermeneutic" which is essentially the interpretation of the faithful gained the greatest consensus approval of the group. The role of liturgy in all its aspects was also considered a vital factor in the common (but not academic) methodology. Although it was nowhere clearly stated, the consensus seemed to focus on the need for getting beyond the present foundations and approaches of exegesis today, as the cardinal stated. This book will be referred to subsequently as *Ratzinger Conference*.

2. Frederick E. Greenspahn, *Scripture in the Jewish and Christian Traditions: Authority, Interpretation, Relevance* (Nashville: Abingdon, 1982), puts the matter well: "If the fact of interpretation testifies to Scripture's authority, the methods used are conditioned by preexisting attitudes about the role the Bible is expected to play; the process of exegesis thus reflects the exegete's own religious conviction"(88). And again: "Methods of exegesis have varied both within and among various traditions....The variety of interpretative methods vividly demonstrates the role of hermeneutics in enabling the exegete to link authoritative Scripture with a reality that might appear to be outside it" (89). Greenspahn's editorial comments on pages 87–90 in this collection of essays by others are well worth reading for our project.

3. Joseph Campbell, *The Hero With a Thousand Faces* (Princeton: Princeton University Press, 1949). This comes into the *Ratzinger Conference*, 114.

4. George Lindbeck in *Ratzinger Conference*, 120.

5. *Ratzinger Conference*, 119–122, "A Disputed Exegetical Establishment," brought out some fairly testy feelings that contemporary interpretation is dictated in university academia by the exegetical establishment of scholars, perhaps as represented by the American Academy of Religion. This is a shift from the church establishment which for many centuries dictated methods and conclusions.

2

Communicating with
Extraterrestrial Intelligence

1. Is Someone Calling?

Carl Steiner sat at his computer console and watched the numbers scrolling down the monitor. They always danced endlessly in this way. The pattern was complicated and yet it kept repeating itself. Carl's title said that he was a research assistant at the Orion Radio-telescope Laboratory for extraterrestrial research.[1] When he had taken the job, he was thrilled by the prospect of being an explorer in outer space. Not that he knew all that much about what he was doing. He had only a basic understanding of computer workings and his knowledge of astronomy was almost limited by what he could see at night. The manager told him that he was an ideal operative; they didn't want him to know too much and risk messing up the job. All he had to do was to observe what the screen said and make notes in a journal.

Professor Hollingwood probed the universe with this array of radio telescopes and all the data was recorded. At some later date other computers would analyze the patterns in the data. Carl was simply a human watchdog to see that the system was working as it should. His shift was only a few hours at a time and mostly he watched for gross malfunctions. But he also kept an eye open for anything unusual in the data itself. Carl understood that this should have been the exciting part of the job, but he found it boring.

So he sat there bored for his fifteen minutes, automatically pacing off the usual run of numbers and the occasional blips. In his active mind he had already run through his baseball schedules, lottery numbers, his last dinner, the shopping list his wife had given him and alternate ways of avoiding traffic on the freeway. He had just decided to take Ubaldi Street home when he became aware that something was odd—some little variation had occurred in the numbers. He had missed it, but it was stored and he could retrieve it later. He restrained himself for the rest of his shift and then moved over to the other terminal to see if he could catch the variant again. He switched back to the beginning of his run and painfully ran through it again. He was right; it did occur. In the endless stream of numbers, 4–3–2 had appeared where it should not have been. He duly recorded the event and the time with a note to his supervisor. What it meant, he had not the slightest idea.

The next day his supervisor gave him a vast amount of print-outs and some very imperative instructions. A scan of the previous recordings had disclosed that for the last five days at exactly 14:31.42 the 4–3–2 had appeared. He was to concentrate each day to see if the odd number appeared at precisely that time. So for the first time something with a little excitement had actually happened, and Carl shared in the thrill, whatever it may have been. Sure enough, on his first day of active watching of the monitor the errant number occurred again. And the next day and the next.

By the end of the week he was summoned to an impressive meeting with people whom he knew to be highly placed radio technicians, computer programmers and astronomers. That was when he learned that his telescope, as he was beginning to think of it, was focused on an errant pulsar in the Milky Way some 25,000 light years away. Some time before a theory had been advanced that this pulsar might possess a planet circling it. It was the first fleeting indication of a planet anywhere in a system other than our own. The evidence for the existence of the planet was a difference of one-hundredth of a second in the rate at which this pulsar delayed or anticipated its beam which came at three times a second. The theory was that the difference was due to a planet circling the pulsar which attracted the beam in a periodic fashion. That had been exciting enough to the technicians although not conclusive. However, this new 4–3–2 variant had nothing to do with that.

The group talked in arcane terms, as far as Carl was concerned, about pulsars and pulses and astronomical distances and mathematical formulae for explaining abnormalities. What he could understand was that 4–3–2 was different. It was not a measure of the regularity or irregularity of the pulsar signal. It was a straight signal which said 4–3–2. Apart from the evident descending order of the numbers there was no hint of what it meant. Mathematical formulas were thrown around, written on the board; philosophies of the meaning of numbers and new starting points for understanding the order of the universe were mentioned. As in any academic discussion, more and more philosophies based on personal suppositions, unrecorded prejudices and sheer whims were strongly proposed and ignored.

James Wittinghaus listened to all of this with a somewhat bemused tolerance. He was the odd man on the committee. He was from the National Academy of the Arts. In deference to the government commission which supplied most of the money, he had been included not as a scientist but as a representative of the humanities. Perhaps one of the old boys on the House committee remembered his classical education and all the mythological names which were associated with planets and stars and thought that somehow they might have something to add to the discussions. So when the technical conversation at the meeting had finally run itself out, someone said half in jest: "Jim, does 4–3–2 mean anything to you?"

"As a matter of fact," he said, "it does. 4-3-2 is a mystic number and you can take that for what you want, but it is one of those recurring numbers in various cultures. 4–3–2 or 4.32 or 432,000 or some other variant, but it always has those three numbers in that order."

"How widespread is this?" somebody asked.

"Well, it's pretty well known," Jim mused much in the fashion of a professor giving a stock answer to a student whom he expected to look up the matter personally. "It was mostly the priestly groups in advanced civilizations who discovered it as a constant in the movements of the heavenly bodies. The Babylonians knew about it and the ancient Hindus called it 'kali yuga' and there are even hints of it in the Bible."[2]

"Was it just an astronomical observation?" somebody inquired.

"No, it went beyond that. At least, that is the way they interpreted it. They applied it to ages of people or of kingdoms. It was something like the Golden Section of the Greeks.[3] You remember that they discovered that if a ratio of 3 to 5 was used to relate height and breadth to a building, such as at the Parthenon in Athens, then you had a pleasing building. Later they discovered that it also applied in some way to music. For some reason they did not understand—and we don't either—it did work."

The Chairman harrumphed a bit and seemed to measure the limits of his tolerance before he said, "Well, Jim, if there is any magic in this gobbledegook which you are suggesting, is there any meaning to the message?"

"Yes, there is," said Jim.

"Well, what is it?" the Chairman said.

"I would rather not tell you," Jim said in perfect professorial fashion. "Look it up for yourselves."

So the meeting came to an end since Jim would not budge, and they were mystified if not bored. 4–3–2 was a message of some sort but the message had to be interpreted in ways which they did not know—and probably would not believe. In fact, even to Carl it was clear that the meaning of the message was not going to be clearly and indisputably revealed. The occurrence of 4–3–2 on the computer data was provable, but beyond that was a leap in the dark which might be based on an ancient myth. Yet the myth seemed to have something more than sheer idiosyncracy to it. It did work.

When Carl got home that evening, he immediately began to scheme how he could find the meaning of 4–3–2. He had nothing at home except books on home carpentry, baseball statistics, "How To Do" this or that, paperback novels which had outlived their endurance. A visit to his local library and a search of encyclopedias under Numbers or Numerology did not yield anything. 1, 5, 7, 10, 40 and multiples thereof were adequately treated, but 4–3–2 escaped him. Since Wittinghaus had mentioned mythology, he had a try at that. Finally, under Assyrian mythology he discovered what he was looking for. 4–3–2 meant the end of an era.

Somebody was sending an SOS. But who were they? And who were the Bad Guys who were causing the trouble? And who were the Good Guys to whom one appealed?

2. Techniques of Story-Telling

This is a standard science fiction story, though hardly up to the better standards. For your consolation it is only a test case for exploring why we are interested in stories about other worlds. Every revealed religion claims that there is a someone out there with whom we can communicate, and so it has more than entertainment value.

How was my story created? First of all, I had a contemporary literary pattern of science fiction which you, the readers, know about. We could both go down the same rails confidently. The distinctive and modern attraction is the stage scenery which comes out of our technological society. Some of that I can supply simply by imagination. But I cannot imagine just anything. We both insist on some reality. Some imaginings will not fit the scientific data—and I may have made mistakes in my little story. That needs to be checked. Indeed, in the movie productions of science fiction it is the scenery which is the most important element, and much of the money gets spent on it and on consultants, design artists and special effects. Although the appeal is basically to the imagination, we want our different worlds to be familiar enough to allow us to understand what is going on.

Eventually what we want to know is whether someone is out there, and then we want to know who it is. Communicating with something or someone out there is as old as literature itself. The first turning point in such a story comes in establishing contact with the "out there." We must have a means of communicating, and then we must interpret first the communication and then the character of the one or ones with whom we are communicating. "Friend or foe?"

Isaac Asimov, one of the best of science fiction writers, once pictured some of his other-worldly creatures in the way artists are inclined to paint ghosts—translucent whiffs with only the hint of a face.[4] They float, they intuit, they seem to be nothing and yet they have personalities. Some of them, the rationals, are only a whiff away from the pure intelligences whom the medieval theologians called angels.

Even earlier, the biblical authors wrote of angels. As the name says, angels were messengers from the "out there." They were usually portrayed as airy creatures. Jacob had a dream at Bethel of a stairway going up to the heavens with God's messengers going up and down (Gn 28:10–12). Many other variants of this story technique occur. Angels often appeared in some human form, and they usually greeted the other people in the story by saying, "Peace be with you." The "friend or foe?" impulse was often there. Somehow people were afraid of or awed by these apparitions. Jesus used the same image of ascending and descending in his conversation with Nathanael; he was the one who went up and down (Jn 1:50–51). It is a theme often repeated in the gospel of John. In the biblical stories the messengers almost always turned out to be friends from "out there." The people who read such stories understood the technique as easily as we understand science fiction.

Nor is the technique confined to the bible; heavenly mediators appear worldwide. The Greeks had Hermes who was the messenger of the gods; sometimes in the ancient Near Eastern world it was prophets or soothsayers; sometimes it was magicians; sometimes it was even symbols or numbers or signs. Sometimes it was people who had died, as in Saul's vision of the ghost of Samuel (1 Sm 28:4–25). The philosopher Plato thought of "souls" as immortal on both ends. The ones who are to live among us are already alive. And of course, reincarnation has been around for a long time in many cultures to explain that we never really die; we simply pass from one form to another. Communication with such beings brings us closer to the whole other world. Bringing it off with a proper mixture of reality and imagination is the crux of the story-teller's art.

3. Characters

Depicting character in the "out there" is more difficult and crucial. The characters, like the scenery, must be understandable enough to convince us that we are dealing with reality. Yet the characters must be revealed as larger than life, larger than our daily worries and petty triumphs, larger than our normal passions, good or bad. Isaac Bashevis Singer, the teller of Jewish folk-tales, once explained his art by saying that God created us with intelligence—not much, but enough to find our way. And with will power—not much, but enough to keep our heads above water. And then God poured gallons and gallons of passion into us. Depicting this well is what makes great literature.

Aristotle thought that only a person of dignity, such as a king, could be a real tragic hero. In Euripides' play *Iphigenia in Aulis* it is the daughter of Agamemnon, the leader of the Greeks against Troy, who is the tragic heroine. She is sacrificed to the gods by her father to get the winds to blow so the fleet can sail. She encapsulates all that is noble in Greek patriotism. The perception of exceptional emotion in characters is what makes for great story-telling since it reveals to us what we truly are.

Our contemporary science fiction tends to be rather weak on character portrayal of the others. Most of them turn out to be rather run-of-the mill clones of humans. On the other hand, the bible and other revealed religions really tell us something that is different about angels, devils, God and us. For example, in the ascending-descending theme in John's gospel we get a fair idea of the Father of us all who gives life and judgment into the hands of his Son.

4. The Plot

Our stories need plots. The casual cops-and-robbers routine will not do for great story-telling. The plot must come to grips with the real problems of human life—its beginning, its end, and the middle in which we live now. It must, in fact, involve us now as readers and yet also as living actors. The great power of story-telling lies in our own engagement in the story. We instinctively see ourselves as characters in the story for good or bad as our TV experience indicates. The story becomes real.

God or whatever one wants to call the extraterrestrial intelligence out there is eventually at the center of the plot, but it is best for the author not to pretend to know too much about that god. The first great science fiction movie, *2001*, probably did a better job by implication than the subsequent productions. At the end Frank Bowman, the surviving astronaut, ages, dies and is reborn.[5] The unseen other is never depicted but is clearly there. That is what we want to know, however obscurely. We do not want to know simply about other intelligences, higher or lower than us, which may be out there. We want to know about "the intelligent one."

So it has always been. The quest for a god out there and for an after-life with the god is found in the most ancient stories which we have. We still hold on to it precariously. According to our polls the great majority of U.S. citizens still believe in an after-life although most cannot go much beyond this. We cannot give cogent proof why this should be. All we know is that we are reacting as other human beings have done. This is the data. Perhaps we cannot stand the thought that we are alone in an impersonal universe. Like orphans seeking their true parents, we want to know where we came from and where we are going. We want to know about a person.

Conflict is always a part of a good story. "They lived happily ever after" is the end of a fairy-tale; our life is different. Perhaps we are always battling with an evil that seems stronger than ourselves and we must have a belief in a good that is even stronger. Such conflict makes for real story-telling.

The great stories which our predecessors handed on to us have a depth and a consistency worldwide which startles us. The stories which have as their topic the great problems of life, the beginning and the projected end, and the expression of this in characters called gods are professionally called "myths." Our popular use of "myth" as the equivalent of "falsehood" is quite different. Myth is professionally distinguished from "legend" which concerns the human hero of a group. In effect, myth is our normal way of expressing theology. Theology, however, must be rational and exist as a system in some way. We have been beguiled by too much involvement in scientific expertise and rational explanation to understand the great stories of the past which still exist among us. But we must understand what we are searching for. The plot we are looking for involves someone out there and some understanding of good and evil. Science fiction has refocused our attention on the "out there," and for that we can be grateful; it is much less successful in picturing the someone who is the necessary central character. But the basic plot of good and evil still holds. What we want our stories to tell can often be found more profoundly in the ancient myths.

This affects our contemporary life. We try to hype ourselves into a rapture for environmentalism and leave it earth-bound with programs to clean up the mess so we can enjoy it. We do not really appreciate the stories of our own American Indians and their reverence for the living Spirit. We don't understand the Spirit or the Great Mother Earth. We have forgotten that there is another way to knowledge than scientific fact or pragmatism.

5. The Appeal of Story-Telling

I began with a science fiction story to introduce some of the techniques or processes which I want to consider in this book. They help us to interpret our spiritual beliefs. We understand science fiction. We know that such stories are largely imaginative. The stage scenery is impressive and we know that some union laborers built it. We insist on some reality. Particularly, the characters and the plot should be realistic, although heightened beyond normal perception. But we cannot ignore the real plot and the real character we are searching for.

Such stories have an abiding persuasive force throughout the course of human life, including our own. We cannot prove the conclusions and they are bewilderingly multiple. But they give us a clue about the technique of going about understanding our story-telling.

In 485 B.C.E. in Syracuse, Greece, a new way of public speaking was first clearly identified. A war had decimated the countryside, and after victory the farmers could not find the markers which set the boundaries for their fields. Understandably, numerous squabbles were generated. The democratic society of Syracuse decided that each farmer would have an opportunity of addressing the *demos* or assembly and they would decide who should get what. In reflecting on the effectiveness of the various presentations, the Syracusans began to recognize that the farmers who won most were not those who had the best cases or the clearest arguments; it was the ones who told the best stories. They carried more persuasion. And so was born the study of rhetoric.

In the classical period of Athens about 300 B.C.E. philosophy and law were separated from rhetoric. Socrates complained of the unfair competition and denounced rhetoricians as frauds. Socrates lost. More people listened to the mythological dramas of the great Greek poets than ever studied Socrates or Aristotle or Plato.

Rhetoric depended on a shrewd understanding of what actually moved people to make decisions. It was not logic in most cases; it was an appeal to something which the hearers instinctively plug into the images in their hidden store of experiences. When the magic words were said, the connection was made although they would not easily recognize why they were acting the way they did.

Rhetoric elaborated itself over the centuries into a complex system of presentation. It did work, however, and so for twenty centuries it was the basis of what we called liberal education. By the 1800s it had become so formalized and intricate that it no longer appealed to the basic instincts and experiences upon which it depended.

In contemporary biblical studies rhetoric has made a comeback, although it is now more commonly called literary criticism. Multiple forms exist and are being tried, from structuralism to deconstructionism to plain old literature study. The precise definition of these methods need not detain us here. What all of them are trying to do is to isolate clues in the document which will tell us what this piece of writing is all about. The clues should normally be evident to the reader as in a good mystery story, or at least they should be recognized once they are pointed out. All of this relies on another supposition which the historical critics such as Bultmann had also recognized—namely, that there is a commonality in the way people react and speak. Languages differ, cultures change, images grow old and unrecognizable, yet the basic appeal remains. But then of course we are not simply interpreting what existed two thousand years ago, but what exists also for us now. We talk about reader-response in literary criticism and really mean how we as the present reader think we should respond. We conceal this in a somewhat clever way by distinguishing between the real reader and the implied reader. But, in fact, we are both. If not, we put the story down.

No text is self-interpreting. The words of the bible exist, but what they mean differs immensely between fundamentalists and strict historians. Something else needs to be added before the text begins to speak to us. Our inherited religious beliefs often determine interpretation; so too do education, culture, identity with a group. The oppressed in our society read the stories in the newspapers about riots or see them on TV in quite a different way than the mainline citizens. The persecuted Christians in Muslim countries read the gospels quite differently than do we in our world. We are often not aware of what that factor is which makes us reach our conclusions. So too scholars justify their work on the basis of facts or methodologies, but their conclusions often seem to come from somewhere else.

ENDNOTES

1. On October 12, 1992 NASA switched on two gigantic radio telescopes in Arecibo, Puerto Rico and in the Mojave Desert of Arizona. They are part of a ten year, $100 million program to listen in on all the radio noises and possibly messages from interstellar space. The Goldstone telescope in Arizona and a tracking station in Australia feed into the All Sky Survey in Pasadena, California to scan the heavens. Two billion radio channels are kept under surveillance. On August 15, 1977 a more primitive telescope at Ohio State University detected the first unexpected signals. Five others have since been heard. *Newsweek,* October 12, 1992.

2. Joseph Campbell, *The Inner Reaches of Outer Space* (New York: Harper & Row, 1988), 35–39 has an interesting section on the 4–3–2 number, including a final footnote that Wilson Sporting Goods developed its long-flight golf ball by computer analysis and found that it had 432 dimples.

3. The Golden Section (cf. McGraw-Hill, *Dictionary of Art*) was developed from the earlier geometric architectural designs in Greece. See also Bernhard Schweitzer, *Greek Geometric Art* (New York: Phaidon, 1971). Such ratios were also applied to music.

4. Isaac Asimov, *The Gods Themselves* (New York: Doubleday, 1972).

5. Arthur C. Clarke, *2001, A Space Odyssey* (New York: Signet, 1968). The novel, which was adapted from the movie, brings out much more clearly the myth of Odysseus, the wayfarer from the Trojan war, in his attempts to reach home. The theme is a common one in mythology; it pictures mankind's attempt to reach the God from whom we came.

3

The Communication

1. Communicating

In 1801 Handsome Lake, a Seneca Indian prophet, convinced his tribe that he had had three visions. The Great Ruler warned them that they must adapt to changed situations which the white man had imposed. They must avoid his vices, but the men must work at farming, abandon individual autonomy and glorification, accept communal order, and with their wives foster family life and their own traditions. For a while great numbers believed Handsome Lake and made him their principal sachem. But then they realized that he was advocating a whole change in accepted customs and that his way of speaking for the Great Spirit was not normal. Handsome Lake went into exile, but those who believed in him persisted, and by 1841 the Code of Handsome Lake was an important force in Iriquois life. It remains so to this day.[1]

The previous chapter noted how stories about communicating with the gods are commonplace. The great religions of the world are all "revealed" religions. They all have some common features of story-telling, but they also claim a distinctive authority. The preceding chapter began with a mini-story of contemporary science fiction. We can imagine such communication with someone out there, the extraterrestrial intelligence, or ETA as it is called in the trade. Our imagining is mostly for our entertainment. Our ancestors were much more serious about it in their religious beliefs, and they had no hesitation about saying God or the gods. The myths of the tribes of earth poses the problem of how they

came to be accepted with a privileged place among their traditions. How shall we evaluate or allow ourselves to be persuaded
by these endless stories, and by our own privileged story? How
shall we have any assurance that anything here is real?

Our contemporary reaction to claims that the story-tellers
heard God speaking is that it is probably a sham. Many such
reports are just that. The ancients were also suspicious, and with
good reason. In the pre-Roman *agora* or plaza of Corinth circa 500
B.C.E. stands the remains of a small temple called "the Oracular
Shrine."[2] Only the foundation and two blocks of the first course of
stones are preserved. Exactly at the center is a place for a small
round altar which stood within a shallow basin connected to the
sacred spring nearby. A tunnel large enough for a man to crawl
through ran underneath. The entrance was concealed by a panel
which exactly matched the neighboring ones. It could not easily
be detected as a door and was kept locked. However, an inscrip-
tion warned the curious away from this door. Inside the tunnel
was another grille. At the far end of the tunnel a small hole, open-
ing out like a megaphone, reached toward the altar. The elaborate
concealment and security suggests that oracles were easily com-
municated by someone within the tunnel. In our skeptical mood
we presume that all oracles are like that.

Yet we should give honest consideration to the way in which
the ancients approached these experiences. We use the word
"manic" without being aware of what the Greeks normally
meant by "mania." They believed that in some ecstatic states a
god had taken over a human being and was speaking through
that person. It was a common idea in ancient times, sometimes
even in the bible. Its dangers were clearly understood. Many of
these oracles, many of the proclamations of the politically
manipulated "false prophets," as the Old Testament called them,
and much of the standard literary presentation were as easily filtered out by the ancients as we do with the commercially moti-
vated PR in our times. Yet there remained a substratum of
experience which could not be dismissed and which the people
accepted as genuine. All the major religions spring from some
such revelation.[3]

The acceptance by the people is the most difficult part to explain. The ancients never had physical proof that the revelation was provable, as our scientific minds would insist. Yet sometimes the message was wholeheartedly accepted and passionately preserved in a written form. How shall we explain this possibly irrational fact?

The same occurs in the bible. The "revealed" communication comes in extremely odd and diverse forms. A prophet like Jeremiah simply said: "Thus says the Lord God..." and people believed. Some of the revealed books of the bible such as Job and Ecclesiastes are apparently fragments of human wonderings about life which escape into divine reflections. They seem to be quite human musings. Some of them such as Proverbs are mostly collections of shrewd folk-sayings. The stories about the kings which we call historical books are termed "the later prophets" by the Israelites, yet they are often dependent on court records. The way in which these revealed data are presented was not decisive for their acceptance.

2. The Reports in Sacred Scriptures

The revealed messages of all the great religions share this quality of mysterious origin. Eventually, the messages were written down and so preserved for the use of following generations. Such are the writings of the Israelite people, of the early Christian communities and the Muslim peoples; so also are the Hindu and Buddhist books of India, the Taoist writings. These constitute the major religions of the world.

Who declared these writings "sacred"? Sacred means separate. They are different from business or entertainment writings or from the wild-eyed visions of fanatics. Most of these records were not only written down, they were preserved with incredible zeal. At Ras Shamra in Lebanon where some of the oldest semitic records have been discovered, the stories of Ba'al and Aqhat and Kirta were preserved in a special library next to the temple. They were all written in a clear script and occasionally signed by a scribe, such as Ilimilku of Shubbani. This clearly sets them apart from the thousands of other tablets discovered else-where at Ras Shamra which run from schoolboy exercises to tax receipts.[4] Certainly there was something different about these tablets concerning the gods which justifies calling them sacred.

What is clear about our sacred scriptures, the bible, is that they were carefully collected and preserved from the time of the final editing. Many of them are rewritings of previous texts. The earliest writings in the bible are probably from before the tenth century B.C.E., such as the song of Miriam in Exodus 15. They were clearly set off from other documents such as those which are noted in the books of Kings as court records and which are no longer extant. In the New Testament we know of letters of Paul which are mentioned but which have disappeared. Whether they were "inspired" or not is beside our point.[5] After the writing of the New Testament, lesser books of commentary or additions to the tradition, such as the *Didache,* the *Shepherd of Hermas* and the *Gospel of Thomas,* were published.[6] Eventually the people decided that these were indeed lesser. Just why the cho-sen books were given such a unique status we do not know, except that they were obviously considered to have some special authority in revealing the relationship of God and the faith group. Often enough they do not sound like God-talk, either as theology, which means talk about God, or as revelation, which means God's communication to us.

If we may judge from the history of our bible which we know best, a pronouncement by authority, civil or religious, does not seem to have originated the choice of these separate or sacred books. That may have happened when additional resources were needed for the preservation of texts which were already fairly definitive. However, it was popular acceptance apparently which governed the decision. People said in effect, "These books express our faith as a people." Later they said: "And these others do not." That usually arose when the accepted books were chal-lenged as a true word of God, or when someone wanted to intro-duce personal ideas as a revelation from God.[7] We call the process canonizing; it resulted in a canon or a list of what was (and so by rejection what was not) considered sacred scripture. It was more than that, as we shall see later, for it was a process which in some general ways interpreted what the books meant.

As noted, we do not know why people accepted some of these books as containing a communication from the extraterrestrial intelligence (and with the eastern religions we cannot really go much beyond that vague phrase). They were not physically different; they were not radically books of prophecy which could be verified by fulfillment; the people who accepted them were not notably more successful than their neighbors; and they were certainly not more rational than the sciences and arts and philosophies which were outside of them. They were accepted simply because this group believed in them—and indeed, in some way, these people were constituted as "this group" mainly because they believed in them.[8] It met a practical need.

Not only did the people define the books; the books defined the people. They felt the need to hang together, often against opposition. They were often persecuted for owning the sacred books. But once again the decision was one of faith. Anyone could just as reasonably have denied that these books were any different from others. But then that could be done only by separating oneself from the group. The separating, however, was also an act of faith since there was no proof that the sacred writings were not revealed or that the group was not needed.

Much of this revealed data comes in story form. The persistence and privileged status of such story-telling within societies embodies a claim to privileged communication of some sort.

3. The Problem of the Mission

First I would note that if the texts we are interpreting were the Gallic wars by Julius Caesar or some Egyptian hieroglyph, all of this would be of not much more than curiosity value. But obviously Christians have taken a more obstinate and determined position on the issue of interpretation of this sacred text than they would about a secular text. They have waged wars, tortured, imprisoned, discriminated in the name of their interpretation. They have made heroic efforts to help neighbors in the most extreme distress, sacrificed their lives for principles, endured cold, boredom, derision for their faith. Today they are divided. On only one point do they seem to agree: this gospel must be preached to all the world—in our way. On that there is no compromise.

Second, it should be noted that the interpretation of this text in its essential values has first been made by the common people, not by the scholars. Scholars have not usually led religious revolutions, but served them. Scholars can sell only such ideas and books as the people will buy. The fundamental interpretation has been "the classic hermeneutic" which George Lindbeck defined as the one which the "nuclear" Christians discover they believe in times of crisis and which they are willing to die for.[9]

Perhaps the description is a bit too much male-oriented. As any pastor knows, the majority of regular participants at church affairs are women. Perhaps they interpret ordinary life as more important; males often need a personal or political crisis to trigger their beliefs. At any rate, interpretation is too important to be left to scholars or simply church leaders.

The people have reached these conclusions in ways which are beyond our scholarly methods.[10] Their sense of identity in belonging to a group has undoubtedly had a great deal to do with their standpoint. The extreme example is fundamentalism. Fundamentalists do not believe on the authority of scholars that they must interpret each word of the bible in a literal sense according to the vernacular translation which they have before them. There is something more important than that, a Resident Alien as interpreter; which is at work because it expresses their whole life outlook. It also allows them to draw up the wagons in a circle when they are attacked.[11]

4. *Interpreting*

In our usual science fiction the message comes from outside our planet in some sort of code, usually mathematical to fit our computer model. We must first decode the message before we know what it says. Only then can we ask: What does it mean?

The writings of revealed religions generally come in well-known languages and have no great need of decoding at that level. However, it soon becomes evident that interpretation is as important as the text itself. The Delphic oracle was the most esteemed in ancient Greece. Its message came in understandable Greek words but they often expressed an enigma. During the war of Athens with the Persians, the oracle prophesied that Athens would be saved by wooden walls and this set the citizens to furious building of new defenses around the city. Pericles, however, saved Athens by reinterpreting the oracle to mean that Athens had to build a fleet to protect itself against the Persians. And so the great battle of Salamis was won. The authority of the oracle and the interpretation were as important as the text. But was the interpretation really honest?

The problem becomes more acute as the messages become more complex. Especially within a canonized set of sacred books, the need for grasping the message as a whole within all the books becomes more crucial. Any individual statement can be interpreted in numerous ways. The total plan of the revelation, however, can be grasped only in its entirety.[12] As Christians we have four gospels, not one. They are not carbon copies of one another, and sometimes they seem sharply divergent. They certainly take different standpoints from which to depict who Jesus Christ was, what he and his followers should do, what this kingdom was of which he talked, etc. The tradition did not homogenize the traditions, although some later Christians tried to do so for liturgical purposes.[13] The tradition canonized the four divergent gospels as the only complete picture.

The literary skill of the gospel writers will not allow us to say that they were unaware of these divergences. Something outside the actual text was already at work which dictated what was authentic and what was not within flexible parameters. This has been true all during the Christian centuries as theologians and historians and story-tellers and poets and artists have interpreted the sacred text. A search for unity and an appreciation of diversity is always at work within the flexible parameters of what we call the "rule of faith."

For example, the presently popular method of literary criticism depends on a pre-formed conviction that there is a commonality in the way in which stories are told in various cultures. It is well substantiated by research, but the theory is not found in the text itself. The previous chapter reviewed various techniques of composing writings, particularly stories. These patterns come before we begin interpreting the text. So also historical criticism begins from an underlying presumption that only facts can be admitted as evidence. Science fiction depends on the tantalizing possibility that the physical descriptions are imaginary but they might be true. It has the same appeal as a "who-done-it?" If the Resident Aliens were not there, we would not be interested in the story.

The intricacies of interpretation are the principal concern of this book. The following chapters will look into some of the elements that go into these unattended assumptions which underlie our interpretation. We shall not arrive at a provable way of interpretation, but we shall perhaps understand better what it is that we are doing.

ENDNOTES

1. Thomas W. Overholt, "Commanding the Prophets: Amos and the Problem of Prophetic Authority," *CBQ* 41 (1979), 517–532.
2. Oscar Broneer, *A Guide to the Excavations of Ancient Corinth* (Athens: American School of Classical Studies at Athens, 1947), 45–49.
3. Jack Finegan, *Light from the Ancient Past* (Princeton: Princeton University Press, 1952), has a list of sacred scriptures from all over. Finegan lists:
   1. Zoroaster (5000; 1200; 500 B.C.E) The texts are called Avesta, twenty-one treatises comprising liturgical teachings, invocations, hymns of praise and a code of purifications and penalties. Manuscripts are from about the ninth century C.E.
   2. Hinduism (1500–1200 B.C.E.) Vedas (four) are the oldest—over a thousand hymns to the gods. Later the Brahmanas or prose commentaries were attached. Later still the Upanishads or "sessions" of teachings, perhaps philosophical meditations, were added. Finally the story of the Mahabharata was inserted and within this is the

famous poem, the Bhagavad-Gita or "Song of the Blessed One." In the Christian period, especially from the fifth to the thirteenth century additional works were composed and added.

3. Jainism. Jainism has a definitive canon of teachings of the Jinas; the first effort at canonization was circa 300 B.C.E. The scripture is known collectively as the Siddhanta. Most of these are instructions or prayers.

4. Buddhism (642–413 B.C.E.) Gautama Buddha lived about 600 B.C.E. The canonical literature is called the Tipitaka (Three Baskets), comprising the Vinayapitaka (discipline), Suttapitaka (discourses) and Abhidhammapitaka (higher exposition). Non-canonical books have been added.

5. Confucianism. The so-called "Confucian canon" dates to between 202 B.C.E. and 200 C.E. It comprises nine books. The first four of the Classics are ascribed directly to Confucius; the Four Books are reports on his sayings.

6. Taoism. Lao Tzu (sixth century B.C.E.?) wrote the Lao Tzu before disappearing from his village across the mountains. The Tao Te Ching was added to this. Apparently these later scriptures were not so definitively canonized as the first.

7. Shintoism. The oldest written sources are the Kojiki or "Record of Ancient Things" and the Nibongi or "Chronicles of Japan." These are mostly legendary tales; real history in Japan begins about the sixth century C.E.

8. Islam. The Qur'an is extremely miscellaneous. The first part presents Muhammad's early preaching; the second has many stories often relying on Judaism and Christianity; the third reflects an anti-Jewish, anti-Christian turning away. These writings were supposedly brought together a year after Muhammad's death; at least, there was an authorized text under Caliph 'Uthman (644–656 C.E.) and other versions were destroyed. The text was preserved with great care. The annexed tradition (it is vast) is called the Hadith.

4. Michael David Coogan, *Stories from Ancient Canaan* (Philadelphia: Westminster, 1978), 10.

5. Albert Sundberg, Jr., "The Bible Canon and the Christian Doctrine of Interpretation," *Interpretation* 29 (1975), 352–371. Sundberg has consistently stressed the chronological and logical priority of "sacred scripture" over "inspired books."

6. The *Didache ("Teaching" of the Twelve Apostles)* is a book of ethical instructions and liturgical regulations from the late first or early sec-

ond century. It influenced much of the subsequent church development. The *Shepherd of Hermas* is an early second century Roman apocalypse which pictured the church as a shepherd guiding Christians through various ethical trials. The *Gospel of Thomas*, which has been much discussed in the public press of late, is a collection of sayings of the "living Jesus" which is usually dated to the beginning of the third century. It is connected with a Gnostic sect in rural Egypt and is claimed by some contemporary scholars to be a source or more accurate record of the sayings of Jesus in the gospels.

7. The crisis provoked by Marcion about 130–160 C.E. is the best Christian illustration of a popular challenge to the sacred books of a group. Marcion organized a Christian church around a small handbook of biblical texts which eliminated the harsh God of the Old Testament, retained only Luke's gospel and concentrated on the letters of Paul as the true apostolic teaching. This popular picture of a nice Jesus who brought only good things captured the allegiance of a large group of Christians which almost overwhelmed the "Great Church." The appeal, however, did not last long, and the traditional body reasserted its acceptance of the Old Testament and the whole apostolic writings from the four gospels to the Apocalypse.

8. Emile Durkheim, the so-called founder of modern sociology, basically argued that religion emerged from a "collective conscience." Religion was established to support and preserve group goals, and it functioned to give such goals sanctity and authority. Cf. Walter H. Capps, *Ways of Understanding Religion* (New York: Macmillan 1972), 92 and the essay of Durkheim which follows. At a later date Jung argued that mythology, like dreams, emerged from group consciousness.

9. George Lindbeck, "Scripture, Consensus, and Community," *This World*, 23 (1988), 5–24 (at 5).

10. George Hopko of St. Vladimir's Theological Seminary was one of the strongest advocates of this view in the *Ratzinger Conference*, 117. For the Orthodox, the liturgy is a primary Resident Alien as is clearly admitted.

11. Gabriel Fackre, "Positive Values and Honorable Intentions: A Critique of Fundamentalism," *New Theology Review*, 1 (1988), 58–71, has an excellent and sympathetic analysis of contemporary fundamentalism which often reacts in this way.

12. James Gustafson, "The Place of Scripture in Christian Ethics: A Methodological Study," *Interpretation*, 24 (1970), 430–455 made the point in a study of reactions to the Vietnam war, and this has become a classic exposition.

13. The *Diatesseran* of Tatian was a second century harmony of the four gospels which came to be widely used in Syria for liturgical readings. By combining all four gospels it intended to give the hearers an overall view of the gospels. Only fragments of it are extant, mostly in a Syrian version. It was quite different from Marcion's truncated New Testament which had a definite theological bias.

4

Myth

1. Stories of Heroes

Hercules was set to accomplish twelve impossible labors. Ovid tells the story of this half-god, half-human. In the eleventh labor he was to bring his wife, Deianira, home. When he came to the river Evenus he found it swollen and guarded by the centaur, Nessus. Hercules entrusted his wife to the centaur to carry her across. Then Hercules himself crossed over, only to find that the centaur was raping his wife. A mighty battle ensued and Heracles slew the Centaur with an arrow.[1]

The book of Genesis tells the story of Jacob struggling with an "angel" at the Jabbok river (Gn 12:3–33). Jacob had gone on a long journey to Mesopotamia to find a wife. He had lived through a whole litany of trials and emerged successful, mostly by his own ingenuity and cleverness. Yet this was not his true character, and he realized that he must return to his homeland to find himself. So he set out for his home in Palestine with a huge retinue of wives, children, servants, cattle, and all the accompaniment.

One great test remained: Would he be permitted to enter his homeland at the frontier? In the gloomy canyon of the Jabbok he ferried his whole family across that dividing line but remained behind himself. That night the river demon came to deny him crossing. Jacob fought with this man or angel as he is variously described, but he could not prevail. Neither could the man. As the sun rose, the demon was forced to leave, for he was the demon of the night. But

34

before he went, he touched Jacob at his thigh and wounded him. Then he also changed Jacob's name to Israel for he "has fought with God and prevailed."

Both of these stories have the same basic elements of the mythological hero story.[2] Both concern a larger-than-life character who has a mission to perform. Both must go on a journey and face seemingly impossible dangers from preternatural foes. Both triumph and enter a new life. The Jacob story is better; Jacob continues to grow and is one of the founders of his people.[3] Hercules (or Herakles in Greek) is a usual Greek tragic figure who at the end is poisoned and dies by the very blood he spilled from the centaur. Technically, we call these legends, i.e., stories about human heroes. The stories about the gods themselves are much more important, but like legends they have their common elements.

2. Stories of the Gods

We have more to learn from the myths than simply the techniques of story-telling. Myths or stories about the gods are found all over the world and from most of the ages we know about. The study of comparative religion is huge and confusing. For our purposes we need to attend to some simple common elements.

First, the religious beliefs of peoples are usually presented as stories. Even when we discover in archeological digs some physical evidence such as a statue or a cult object, we know that there is a story behind it. Second, Aristotle said a very simple but profound thing. Every story has a beginning, a middle and an end. That is true of the stories of the gods. The beginning is always some story of "creation," and that defines who we are and what our task is. The end, often an impressive cataclysm called an apocalypse, pictures where we are going. The middle is where we live now between birth and death, amid cosmic forces which we understand only vaguely and which we even less control. It is a time of conflict, largely between life and destruction. Life is experienced in the growing of the crops, the begetting of babies, the building of cities to preserve art and language and technol-

ogy; destruction is war, famine, and especially personal human
conflict. The middle must connect the beginning and the end in
the story. The local coloring of the stories changes endlessly
according to place and time, but the substantial plot from beginning to end remains.

Joseph Campbell has argued in *The Hero with a Thousand Faces*
that the essential plot is one of salvation.[4] By "hero" Campbell
means a god-like figure who comes into our world. "A hero ven-
tures forth from the world of common day into a region of supernatural wonder: fabulous forces are there encountered and a
decisive victory is won: the hero comes back from this mysterious adventure with the power to bestow boons on his fellow
men."[5] In the middle of the story we have the kind of conflict
which we know from our daily experience, and we realize that
our only escape is by the hero coming into the story from the
land of the gods to save us. His coming is sometimes secret; his
career may be a long series of hair-raising exploits against a
determined foe; often the hero is killed. But he comes back to life.
Campbell remarks: "There's a certain type of myth which one
might call the vision quest, going in quest of a boon, a vision,
which has the same form in every mythology."[6] Later he says:
"…there is a certain typical hero sequence of actions which can
be detected in stories from all over the world and from many
periods of history. Essentially, it might even be said there is but
one archetypal mythic hero whose life has been replicated in
many lands by many, many people. A mythical hero is usually
the founder of something—the founder of a new age, the
founder of a new religion, the founder of a new city, the founder
of a new way of life. In order to found something new, one has to
leave the old and go in quest of the seed idea, a germinal idea
that will have the potentiality of bringing forth that new thing."[7]

As with all opinions of scholars, this one is not universally
accepted. Yet oddly when scholars are required to explain their
findings popularly, they almost always arrange their books on
the pattern of creation/conflict/after-life.[8] What is obvious is that
the scholar must have some unifying theme for the study or else
the book cannot be written. The probabilities for Campbell's con-

clusion seem great. So also if one asks where this agreement in the records, total or merely widespread, came from, we have more divergent opinions. Some would say that there was an original story somewhere from which all the others borrowed. Eventually that leads through various types of religious belief—animism, magic, polytheism, and so to a current ethical monotheism—for which an historical and developing pattern must be discerned. This is the school of comparative religion, and it is not always in agreement about this.[9] Others, such as Carl Jung the psychologist, would say that we have something innate in us, an archetype, a collective conscious or something that can be detected within the structure of myth.[10] So we have a structural school.

How does one decide today between two such sophisticated views? More study is helpful, but neither of the two schools is able to prove its point conclusively. Whatever conclusion one reaches is not based on pure logic or proof. We make a decision on faith of some kind that one is more probable than the others. Or we believe that there is nothing in any of them. Oddly enough, whatever we do must be done on faith of some sort. No one of the explanations ever conquered all the rest by logic or political conquest. The wisest of the conquerors simply let people hold on to their old gods as long as they accepted the new ones also. So why did people in any one place or time decide that this was the story they would tell about beginnings or endings or in-betweens? Some decision was made on faith. As we look back now, we discover that the faith in such divergent stories has a consistency about the basic plot. But we do not know why, except that it seems human to do so if we may accept our experience as a race.

To get back to our analogy of the science fiction story, all of these myths are claims for communication with some extraterrestrial intelligence. They are stories about the gods which somebody presumably heard and which said something to them about how they were involved with the gods. If they are not products of the imagination, the details of the story are strongly influenced by imagination. Yet they were also based on reality, the street-wise admission that we could not cure our own ills and needed salvation.

It is imagination alone which can span the unknown "above" for answers which logic or science or academic methods cannot. The imagination is expressed in some definite form and function; it is not an abstract proposition. It is familiar to us from our everyday life. It differs from place to place and time to time as our everyday life does. Hence the hero has a thousand faces.

Studies of mythology present us with this as data. In science fiction we begin by imagining mysterious signals from space which come through radio waves and computers. As the plot develops, however, the data usually gets interpreted as a limited conflict of good and evil which is similar to what we know on planet earth. But myths go far beyond that toward some involvement of a cosmic plot and a cosmic hero who brings total salvation.

The problem here centers on the interpretation of what the communication means. The myths are not simply "entertainments," as Graham Greene called his novels or as most of our science fiction movies are. Myths are clearly important for establishing the identity of a group. Indeed this is central.

3. Identifying

Whatever else may be said about these myths, we instinctively refer to them both popularly and in scholarly terms as myths of the Egyptians or Assyrians or Navajos or Puma Indians, etc. They are "myths of the..." We identify them by a name of the group among whom we found them. Scholars call these cultural units "monads," i.e., identifiable social groups which stick together.[11] But we are back to the "chicken-and-the-egg" problem. Which came first? The group or the myth? Did the group make the myth or did the myth coalesce the hearers into the group? As far as we know, the earliest humans lived in cooperative families. The earliest evidences of myths also come from a cooperative group. Apparently the myths made the group stick together.

Myth clearly is a way of unifying the group and taking advantage of what has been found helpful in the cooperative living. It passes on the lore of experience by way of story and gives understandings of it.[12] Certainly in later recorded history, as we know it, the myth was most important as the cement which held the group together, especially in competition with other groups.

The tribes of Israel were simply a disparate group of oppressed peoples in Egypt until they rediscovered their traditional religion.[13] Freedom of religion or "pluralism" was not a highly regarded virtue in the world from which so many of our stories come. Most often political conquest led to the imposition of foreign myths upon a people. However, amalgamation of stories also went on endlessly through either travel or commerce; the gods of one group were accepted by another but their own were not forgotten. Usually, they were simply spliced in somewhat haphazardly. We talk of a Graeco-Roman culture, and the myths of both groups are so intertwined that it is difficult at times to tell where one began and the other ended; many of the gods have different Greek or Latin names although they are clearly the same god. A logical or consistent synthesis of the details apparently was not needed. What was needed was some consistent master story.

Azhura-Mazda's story in Mesopotamia held together vast numbers of peoples. It was a distinctive story of good and evil gods existing on an equal basis. Buddhism came to dominate India—but only for a while. Islam dominated the Arab world, and although it spread beyond the Arabs, it had definite geographical limits. The Sioux Indians had stories about a single deity, the Great Spirit Wakantaka. The Huron myth is more elaborate. The goddess Ataentsic fell from heaven when she became pregnant and gave birth to the twins, Turtle and Muskrat. They were the beginning of our present world. The Greeks and Romans also had notions of such twin progenitors, but there is no connection between the Graeco-Romans and the Hurons. Indeed, the basic story plot is fairly common. There seem to be definite geographical limits to the groups which held stories in common, and the limits were defined by specific conditions under which people lived. Yet there were common elements to the stories within different sociological groupings.

The quality of the myths tended to be localized largely by the immediate living conditions of the believers. That Egyptians who lived in a sunny land with the Nile as a dependable source of water and fertility should have honored Ra, the sun, and have cherished the orderly life is understandable. That the Assyrians who lived in present-day Iraq where conditions were much more harsh by nature and much less defensible by natural boundaries should have had warlike and predatory gods is also understandable. The hunter peoples who were at home with animals tended to express their beliefs in pictures of animals which they drew; the farmers made icons of fertility goddesses; the fisher-folk were in awe of giant fish and dragons. This would be immediately understandable.

However, it went farther than this. Within specific living areas the differences continued. Village differed from village. When we speak of African Christianity today we glorify inculturalization. In practice we then discover that the culture is subdivided into such small segments that it is difficult to adapt any universal symbol or liturgy to disparate local needs. Many a missionary in Africa has been thwarted by working out a Christian liturgy which fits local customs only to find that it does not appeal to people in the next mission. The symbols and liturgies express the universal theological ideas; the native culture expresses the differences which identify this one local group. Empire building, both in the ancient world as well as in our contemporary one, demands such plurality. But then the basis for holding people together becomes very slim. "One world" is a marvelous idea, and the great religions all have it; obviously it is difficult to establish identity on that level.

The situation is not altogether different among us. Andrew Greeley in his study of American Catholics since Vatican Council II discovered by sociological sampling that a good number of liberal Catholics were returning to worship in their old church.[14] They had not changed their liberal views nor reconciled them with what they thought was official church teaching. But they did feel out in the cold. It is very difficult for such people to experience identity beyond specific causes. Apparently the returnees valued identity above vindication of their own rightness.

The world of myth is full of violence. So also is the real world. Survival depends on commitment. In the world which lived by recognized myths, there were no survivors among the pacifists or unbelievers.[15] Those who did not cling to their myth disintegrated against the invasions of "religious fanatics," if one must put it in the extreme. "Yahweh is the great king" was thunder stolen by the Israelites from hostile neighbors in Assyria. "Allah is Allah and Muhammad is his prophet" was the rallying cry of Muslims. "Jesus is the Lord" was the absolute test for the Christians.[16] The myths always ended with an apocalyptic vision of the survival of the chosen. The logical and philosophical religions never generated a popular support group.

4. The Problem of History

The problem with mythology occurs when it is used as an exclusive criterion for explaining religion. The mythic world is a never-never land of necessary imaginings. It has great insight and truth which cannot be expressed otherwise. Every once in a while myth crosses history and a crisis of interpretation occurs. As long as the gods are in their timeless world, we can see them as shadow figures of realities in our world. But if they enter our human world at a definite time and place, then we do not quite know what to do with them. We can bend myth to become legend. So the Greeks made some of their traditional human heroes, such as Herakles, into gods. That was long after the historical figure had lived and these heroes never attained the rank of major gods. We can also create the beginning of the mythic story by having the gods born into our society, often by some virgin-birth story. But to have ordinary historical facts intermingle with the myths has involved us in some of the most perplexing problems.

In the Jacob story, for example, we have a curious intermingling of myth and history. The story of the struggle with a god is common enough. Jacob does not become a god nor does he see the god, but he comes close. He is a hero, and the story is really a legend about a human hero. On the other hand, the story has some root in the essential history of Israel. Without a connective between God and Abraham, the plot of the later stories of Moses, Isaac and Jacob and the subsequent history breaks down. Just how much history is here we cannot say, but there is some. We usually call it an "historical nucleus," vague though that is. That these things happened precisely as described is unlikely, but that there was a Jacob-hero in the line of ancestors is vital for the salvation myth. The story as story is important theologically to emphasize that Jacob acquired a new life by contending with God and eventually admitting that he could not conquer God. He was not the savior.

So now we have two sorts of data. One is the data of mythological or legendary imagination which is in the story; another is the data of actual occurrence. Both need to be interpreted and without confusing them. This is a work of artistry, like a sculptor summoning the image hidden in the brute stone to come forth into life. The final image is a work of art which needs to be interpreted according to its finished form. But the product is also dependent on the facts of the kind of marble which was used, the tools which were available, the expense involved, the training and genius of the artist.

This has been the problem of the presently accepted historical criticism in the interpretation of the biblical text. Historical criticism has great strength and value, but is often in danger of interpreting the data simply on the physical basis of whether stories really happened; mythological interpretation makes the mistake of interpreting exclusively on the basis of imagination. We must have both, but each in its proper sphere. We shall next look at how scientific scholarship goes about its work.

ENDNOTES

1. Ovid, *Metamorphoses*, ix, 62–86. Brookes More, *Ovid's Metamorphoses* (Francestown: Marshall Jones, 1941), 404–406.
2. Theodor H. Gaster, *Myth, Legend, and Custom in the Old Testament*

(New York: Harper & Row, 1969), 205–211. Gaster is the best known commentator on Sir James G. Frazer's classic *Golden Bough* from a biblical viewpoint. His Introduction, which deals with folklore and the Old Testament, is well worth reading.

3. The Jacob story ends many chapters later (Gn 49:1–27) when Jacob has become an old man and has learned that God has been in control of all the events of his life. At the end of the story the editor has included a lengthy "prophecy" about the future of his twelve sons.

4. Joseph Campbell, *The Hero with a Thousand Faces* (Princeton: Princeton University Press, 1949).

5. Joseph Campbell, *The Hero with a Thousand Faces* (Princeton: Princeton University Press, 1949), 30. Campbell elaborates on this monomyth: "The first great stage [is] that of *separation or departure....*" Then comes: "The *return and reintegration with society*, which is indispensable to the continuous circulation of spiritual energy into the world, and which, from the standpoint of the community, is the justification of the long retreat, the hero himself may find the most difficult requirement of all" (36). It is this stage which brings salvation. "The composite hero of the monomyth is a personage of exceptional gifts. Frequently he is honored by his society, frequently unrecognized or disdained. He and/or the world in which he finds himself suffers from a symbolical deficiency. In fairy tales this may be as slight as the lack of a certain golden ring, whereas in apocalyptic vision the physical and spiritual life of the whole earth can be represented as fallen, or on the point of falling into ruin" (37). "The cosmogonic cycle is presented with astonishing consistency in the sacred writings of all the continents, and it gives to the adventure of the hero a new and interesting turn; for now it appears that the perilous journey was a labor not of attainment but of reattainment, not discovery but rediscovery. The godly powers sought and dangerously won are revealed to have been within the heart of the hero all the time. He is 'the king's son' who has come to know who he is and therewith has entered into the exercise of his proper power—'God's son' who has learned to know how much this title means. From this point of view the hero is symbolical of that divine creative and redemptive image which is hidden within us all, only waiting to be known and rendered into life" (39). This is the thesis which Campbell illustrates in detail in the rest of the book.

6. Campbell, *The Power of Myth*, 129. Campbell develops much the same idea in *The Inner Reaches of Outer Space: Metaphor as Myth and as Religion* (New York: Harper & Row, 1988). Here, he clearly adopts the

approach of C.E. Jung on "archetypes of the unconscious" or the "elementary ideas" of Mircea Eliade. At the end he alludes to Eliade's "ethnic idea" which is the specific, local, or historical form in which these elementary ideas are situated.

7. Campbell, *Power*, 136.

8. *Myths* by Mircea Eliade, Joseph Campbell, and Alexander Eliot (New York: McGraw-Hill, 1976) is an impressive "coffee-table" book. It begins with the creation and then the death myths. In between are magic, animals, lovers, combat and distant quests. Joseph Campbell with Bill Moyers, *The Power of Myth* (New York: Doubleday, 1988), was a best-seller following a Public Broadcasting Company television series. It, too, begins with the story-tellers of creation and ends with the masks of eternity. In between is sacrifice, the hero, the goddess and love.

9. Cf. Mircea Eliade, *The Sacred and the Profane: The Nature of Religion* (New York: Harcourt, Brace, Jovanovich, 1959), 216–232, for a survey of the history of religion as a branch of knowledge.

10. Joseph Campbell thinks that Carl Jung's "collective conscious" of the archetypes is the best explanation for the consistencies. Cf. also *Power*, 51.

11. In *Inner Reaches* Joseph Campbell refers to "monad" as "not a function of the number and character of such influences and details, but of the psychological stance in relation to their universe of the people, whether great or small, of whom the monad is the cohering life" (12).

12. Gerald A. Larue, *Ancient Myth and Modern Man* (Englewood Cliffs: Prentice-Hall, 1975), devotes a chapter to "Societal Myth" beginning with primitive times (64–67) and then considers historical times in Egypt, Mesopotamia, the bible, Zoroaster, etc. In fact, this is the central idea of his book (pp. 64–130). Joseph Campbell, *The Inner Reaches of Outer Space* (New York: Harper & Row, 1988), refers to myth as a control system: "Thus a mythology is a control system, on the one hand framing its community to accord with an intuited order of nature and, on the other hand, by means of its symbolic pedagogic rites, conducting individuals through the ineluctable psychophysiological stages of transformation of a human lifetime—birth, childhood and adolescence, age, old age, and the release of death—in unbroken accord simultaneously with the requirements of this world and the rapture of participation in a manner of being beyond time" (20). The function of myth as identifying does not seem to be treated extensively by mythologists, but seems to be taken for granted by them.

13. Norman K. Gottwald, *The Tribes of Yahweh: A Sociology of the Religion of Liberated Israel, 1250–1050 B.C.* (New York: Maryknoll, 1979), made this the thesis of his study of the biblical Israelites. To Gottwald it was not only the initial rallying of some Egyptians (we may as well call them that, since they had been in Egypt for centuries) around Moses but the later accretions of Palestinian peasants who revolted against a feudal system and joined the invaders. It was the common adoption of traditional stories of varied kinds which was the cement that held these disparate peoples together.

14. Andrew M. Greeley, *American Catholics Since the Council: An Unauthorized Report* (Chicago: Thomas More, 1985), 77–79. In assessing the data on church attendance after Vatican II, Greeley concludes that "In the middle nineteen-eighties the majority of church attenders (four-fifths) reject the birth control encyclical and yet continue to 'align' themselves to Sunday because of a loyalty....They justify this loyalty by an appeal to the love of God over against the authority of the institutional church." In summary, he adds: "All that can be said at the present state of our knowledge about the decline in church attendance between 1969 and 1975 is that it was sharp, it was sudden, it was related to sexuality, its effect was inhibited by loyalty and by a certain kind of religious imagery, and it is now over."

15. Joseph Campbell does a good job at explaining the universality of myth as archetypical imaginations in *The Inner Reaches of Outer Space* (New York: Harper & Row, 1988), 27–51, "Cosmology and the Mythic Imagination." He goes through the transcendence/immanence factor, father/mother, warrior god/life-giver, etc., although oddly he attributes the emergence of evil to Ahzura-Mazda dualism as validation for subsequent conflict. He recognizes that all the local variants are due to factual matters of geography, social change and history, but he cannot really make a convincing case for the real historical facts.

16. 1 Cor 12:2: "Therefore, I tell you that nobody speaking by the Spirit of God says, 'Jesus be accursed.' And no one can say, 'Jesus is Lord,' except by the Holy Spirit."

5

Scientific Interpretation

1. The Affair of Harold Wiggins

Since much of our present interpretation of the bible is professedly scientific, I would like to give something of an insider's view of what goes on. Perhaps it will be a bit of a caricature, but basically it is a slice of reality.

Harold Wiggins strode with determined pace through the hot summer afternoon as he made his way to the library. He was hotter inside than out, however. That a mere layman should challenge him—he, Professor Wiggins, nationally known if not yet internationally, as a preeminent New Testament scholar! And Faraday—a simple-minded seller of used cars had dared to contradict the obviously insightful answer which he had given to such a basic question. Wiggins harrumphed, ignored the students who greeted him and almost walked through the glass doors of the library.

It was a crucial question all right, and it had been some years since he had examined it in detail. The text was: "The just man lives by faith." Faraday thought that it referred to his boundless confidence in himself as a used car salesman and that the church-going bit was just a little PR dressing for the trade. Wash the tires on the car so that the prospects could kick them with confidence. Any salesman knew that; it was in the same category as this religious blah-blah.

So Wiggins strode determinedly to the Greek texts and pulled down the United Bible Society New Testament critical edition. There were others, and although they were largely alike, Wiggins was a connoisseur and wanted only the best. As he suspected there were no variants in Romans 1:17. But who was a "dikaios," a just one? And what was "pistis," faith? And what did "live" mean? Did it refer to what one did during a day? Or did it refer to some kind of special life which God gave? Wiggins was a bit rusty, but as a professional he knew where to go. TDNT (as a professional he dispensed with the title *Theological Dictionary of the New Testament*) had pages and pages of information on these words. It traced their developments and uncertainties through their original Greek meanings, into the cognate Hebrew ones and then began to discuss at length the meanings which they had in various biblical passages. Of course, the meanings changed somewhat from century to century and area to area. Wiggins also knew that he was reading somebody else's interpretation when he got that far, and he did not quite trust it.

There was, for example, how this sentence should be interpreted in the light of Habakkuk 2:4 where it was originally written in Hebrew. A good deal of controversy hinged on that preliminary step depending on whether one was content with a simple historical meaning of this single text or whether one connected it with previous hints of the same observation (or prediction?) in other prophets and whether one interpreted it within a prophetic saying category or within an apocalyptic setting. Was it: "The man who is just will live"? or "The man who is just will survive this destruction of Jerusalem"? or was it a general observation that the one who listens to the prophet will be just and live in a spiritual way by the power of the law of the Lord? Or were there other meanings?

Wiggins decided he would go along with the power of the Lord idea. That dumbbell Faraday had no idea that the text might mean anything like that and that was why he was a used car salesman. However, there was a problem. Could one take an interpretation from the Old Testament and apply it immediately to the New Testament usage?

Was that the way Paul worked? It wasn't the way Matthew did things and it might not be Paul's way. But Wiggins had enough general knowledge of that to shy away from any simplistic views. He would need to analyze the whole context of the epistle to the Romans since Paul used this as his keynote phrase.

So he started with the classic interpretations of Paul— Bultmann's great commentary and Karl Barth's very distinctive one and Kasemann. Then he got down to the lightweights. However, although there was much good insight, there was very little agreement. By chance he came across Hans Deiter Betz and his "forensic rhetoric" approach. At that point Wiggins knew that the opposition had switched pitchers on him. The "classics" were all from an historical criticism viewpoint; Deiter Betz was into this revived rhetorical criticism.

Wiggins found Deiter Betz interesting, but he was in a strange world. When he started to probe deeper, Wiggins had to wade through Levi-Strauss and Derrida and the lesser samples found in various journals. "Reader-response" became an issue. But which reader was to give the response? The ones in Rome to whom Paul presumably sent the letter or people like Wiggins and Faraday today? How could one discover what response Paul had intended? Nobody could look into his mind. To be scientific and objective, one had to stick to the text for indications. Those tended to go in different ways according as one accepted different methodologies of literary interpretation. Some critics even claimed that language never had one, univocal meaning, and so the text might actually be interpreting something which was already in the reader. And what would happen if he began with mythology? Paul, after all, took for granted that readers knew the story of Jesus. Did they and he interpret the story of Jesus in the light of the universal hero myth?

Four days later Wiggins went home with a briefcase full of papers. He sat down at his computer and began composing the final and definitive interpretation of these six words which had gotten him started. His logic was impeccable. Harold Wiggins, Ph.D. from Harvard, male, Presbyterian, slightly more than middle-class, divorced with two sons, old Scottish background, had arrived at the critical and scientific explanation he sought. And he was content with his expertise. But in the dark of the night he knew that he was kicking tires.

2. On the Trail of the Authentic Meaning

The above story is an abbreviated and somewhat caricatured account of what scripture scholars often actually do. I use it as a starter simply to point out the enormous number of instinctive faith decisions which must be made in this kind of scientific study. Then I shall try to evaluate where it ends. Those of us in the trade are aware that we have more expertise in limited areas than in others. We can't do it all ourselves, so we trust the specialists. This chapter simply investigates some of the formal decisions which such work involves. The next chapter will deal with the personal side of the decisions as exemplified in the first great interpreter, Paul. Yet the two cannot really be separated, and I have tried to include in my story at the beginning of this chapter those touches of human resentment and prejudice and zeal which inevitably enter in.

3. Some Problems with Ancient Writings

Much of the scientific investigation of the bible in our Western world has arisen over the centuries and is well-known. Like any scientific study it has its basics and its sophistications. The basics begin with the texts and the languages themselves. The Judaeo-Christian scriptures have been handed down in written form for probably three thousand years since the earliest poems were written. In the course of the centuries, in handwritten texts especially, endless variants have occurred, some deliberate and some simply errors. Some letters in any alphabet look alike and can be confused. Much of the writing was done by professional scribes in a factory and later in monasteries. A master read the text and each scribe wrote it down as he heard it. There was quality control exercised when the scribes submitted the day's work for their pay. Nonetheless errors did creep in. Then there were the more sophisticated scribes or commentators who corrected the manuscripts for what they thought was style or clarity of thought or some favorite idea. Mark's gospel, for example, has three endings which clearly indicate that various copyists made changes to smooth over the abrupt ending which they found.

Errors once made tended to be repeated in subsequent copies, and they spawned more in turn. In New Testament manuscripts we can make some reasonable divisions into families of manuscripts which display much the same variants. We can even make some fairly secure evaluation of what the first copy looked like. Yet some doubt remains. None of our manuscripts go back as far as the first century. The earliest complete New Testament dates to the fourth century C.E. Before that we have only fragments and hardly anything older than 150 C.E. The Hebrew manuscripts of the Old Testament are considerably younger, mostly dating from the ninth century C.E., except for the Dead Sea Scrolls which date from the first century B.C.E. until the end of the first century C.E.

Despite the enormous number of variant readings which can be found in the critical apparatus of any text in the original languages, the accuracy of the copyists' work in the sacred scriptures is astounding. When the Dead Sea manuscripts were discovered at Qumran, we found that they agreed substantially with the Hebrew manuscripts which were a thousand years later. Presumably the accuracy of transmission was somewhat similar in the centuries which preceded Qumran. No other ancient manuscripts which have been handed down in copies show anything near the degree of accuracy of the bible. At any rate, this is a work for experts on whom most of us must rely at least for assistance.

But then we must contend with the meaning of the words themselves. Words are defined in dictionaries by studying how they are used in multiple documents and speech patterns. Sometimes this is fairly simple when we are dealing with basic physical things, such as tables and doors. The abstractions, however, tend to develop multiple meanings and sometimes to reverse themselves. In English the word "prevent" early on meant to "go before"; now it means to stop something before it happens. We need to study the history of the development of the meaning of words to be sure that we have the right meaning for the right historical period. "Wisdom" meant a workman's skill in early Greek; by the time of the New Testament it meant a deep understanding of what underlay the affairs of living. Only for a relatively brief time in the golden age of Athenian learning did it clearly mean philosophy—an English word which comes from the Greek "love" and "wisdom." This is a well-known word which occurs many times in ancient secular writings. We have more difficulty with unusual words or words which do not occur outside the New Testament. Just how accurate we are in these determinations depends on how much evidence of similar words we have in the ancient sources.

Most perplexing are the connotations of words. We have all been puzzled when someone who is not from our region speaks English and puts a different slant on it. We know how words can be made to have different meanings as they are pronounced in certain ways. The written text often has no way of indicating this. Presently no one speaks biblical Hebrew or common Greek in the way the biblical peoples spoke them. We can never quite be sure that we are picking up the proper nuance; we don't speak the languages as natives.

So also the grammar of a sentence can be understood in different ways. Especially in a highly inflected language like Greek where sentences can run to great length, the possibilities of variant interpretations are heightened. We have rather accurate grammars of Hebrew, Aramaic and Greek these days, but we still do not have answers to all the perplexities. This too is a very specialized field in which the usual scholar must depend on others.

4. Structuralist Interpretation

How does language convey meaning? Languages appear immensely different in sight and sound; it is laborious to learn a new one especially if it is of a different family. Yet the structuralists claim that all languages have the same basic structure and only the visual or aural signs differ.[1] Structuralism is not particularly a biblical discipline and applies to any kind of communication, not only writing or the bible. The claim of structuralists is that its method is an interpretative tool. The application of this principle leads to an understanding of the "deep meaning" which is really conveyed by the structures which neither the writer nor the reader probably adverts to but which in fact govern what they are communicating. This commonality is somewhat similar to what we claim for myth. People hear a mythological story and are intent upon the story; it takes reflection to recognize that there is a basic pattern behind the story which is the real meaning. Such also is the structuralists' claim.

The theory has been applied to biblical texts; the practical application often leaves much to be desired in many scholars' minds. Yet the principle of intrinsic structures has an appeal. However, there is no way to prove that the principle is correct or that the conclusions reached by applying it are more objective than others. We take that on faith.

5. Reader-Response Critics

In literary criticism, "reader-response" criticism seems to have spun off from this in quite another way. If two of us go to a movie and one is enthusiastic and the other bored, we have two different subject-responses. If all we can say is: "Well, I liked it" or "I didn't," we don't have much to talk about. We may begin to analyze the other person: "You only say that because you always cry at a sad movie." Perhaps what we say reveals more about who we are more than about the movie. The new hermeneutic school coined the saying that the text interprets the reader rather than the other way around. If so, then there is something already in the reader which is being interpreted.

Centuries ago Aristotle observed that in any written work we have the author, the text and the reader. Of these, he said, the reader is the most important. Whatever the writer intended or the words said, the meaning conveyed is that which the reader gets out of it. There is no right or wrong about that; it may be a misunderstanding, but that is what the reader got. Indeed, there may be multiple (sometimes indefinitely so) meanings as there are multiple readers. That this is a fact of life seems indisputable, but in this extreme form it leaves us without any ability to talk about what the text really means. It means what it means to you and that is that.

Whatever structuralism and reader-response can tell us, it is clear that we must make multiple acts of faith as we use the methods. We are using these techniques in order to interpret how the author tried to communicate and in how the reader is expected to understand. We are certainly a long way from being objective. That was the same problem we encountered in historical criticism.

6. Taking History Seriously

Many have quoted Alasdair MacIntyre's saying: "Fact is an invention, along with the waistcoat and men's wigs, of English gentlemen of the eighteenth century."[2] We did not always think of facts as the only proof. In the historicist's view, the meaning of an event is fairly well exhausted if it tells what actually happened. In the extreme version of historical criticism any other test is irrelevant. Eventually this provoked the continuing crisis in biblical interpretation which centered around the "historical Jesus" versus the "Jesus of faith."[3]

As historical criticism of the bible gained credence in the nineteenth and twentieth centuries, source criticism and form criticism revealed something of the history of development of the text. That, in fact, is what the original German term *heilsgeschichte*, form-history, meant to historical critics. We had pushed the seemingly straightforward gospel accounts into much later teaching-shaped versions, sometimes called kerygma or "preaching of salvation." As such, they were accurate historical records of the faith of the early churches. But whether there ever was a real man, the Jesus who said and did all of these things, was persistently questioned. The faith of the early church was a fact, but the historical Jesus could not be excavated from the later literary overburden. Sometimes the reader-response of the critics was to question whether the whole story had simply been made up.

Nikos Kazantzakis in his *The Last Temptation of Christ* created a marvelous bit of irony at the end of his story which captured the rationalistic attitude of the late nineteenth and early twentieth centuries. In dream-like climax of the story, Kazantzakis presumed that Jesus had never died and after recuperating from his wounds married Mary Magdalene and was a happy father. One day he heard Paul preaching in his village the fiery message of salvation through the risen messiah. Jesus took Paul aside and tried to tell him the truth: he had never died. And Paul said: "True or false—what do I care! It's enough if the world is saved!"[4] The drama is high.

With such a limited view of truth, the conflict of extreme historical criticism with established faiths was unavoidable.[5] Bultmann sought to avoid it by claiming that the true meaning could be found by "demythologizing." More recent approaches such as reader-response criticism attempt to shift the real meaning to the reader and so leave historical truth irrelevant as far as the method goes. Sometimes now we hear a plea on several fronts for a new age in which truth will not be measured by any of the specific determinants which produced myth or history or doctrine or tradition. We shall have freed ourselves from these petty claims and immersed ourselves in the All-Being. This is perhaps the greatest faith statement of all.

The problem, of course, is that these approaches demand faith in far more things than even a fundamentalist would dare claim. Must one then believe that the underlying structures exist as described, that fact and reality have nothing to do with the sacred scriptures of the world, and that whatever future is predicted by science is the real one?

7. Scholarly Conflicts

For the past century the most common way of interpreting the bible among scholars (and now often among others) has been historical criticism. Historical criticism at its extreme puts its faith in facts as the only truth. Even when we don't believe the picture which is produced, we are still mesmerized by it since it seems "real." The renewed interest in the historical Jesus indicates our continuing desire to find something important in the history, as indeed we must. The attitude seems to say that only from the facts can one begin a reasonable discourse. So a great deal of effort has been given over the past century to discovering facts, first the physical facts of archaeology, geography and social conditions, and later the facts about the sources of the biblical materials, their development during the period of composition and lately the basic themes which govern the final edition. Not much attention is paid to the interpretations which began immediately after the biblical period down to modern times. It is rare to find references to the fathers or medieval scholars in modern commentaries.

In the historical approach a problem arises about time. History necessarily demands a time frame, a chronology of exactly when events happened. Supposedly we are investigating the events of two thousand years ago. In the expression of the historical critics we are interested in the "living situation" at the stage of development which we are investigating. But are we using our own kind of contemporary interpretation, aided by computer programs of sociological models, in that antiquarian quest to reach a our conclusion? Our own "living situation" is not far below the surface.

Most of the scholars who do the interpreting are associated with some Christian or Jewish denomination; perhaps their jobs depend on it. It is not entirely an impersonal or an objective exercise, free from pressures or compulsions.[6] Moreover a conformist

attitude is exerted on scholars in the United States by professional associations such as the American Academy of Religion
and by the accrediting agencies.[7] So whose time are we talking
about when we interpret—theirs or ours, then or now?

Rudolf Bultmann, the foremost proponent of historical criticism, was aware of the problem of giving a personal meaning to
the bible. In one way he tried to follow Heidegger and his search
for authentic being. In another way he tried to close the gap
between the then and now by a theory of "demythologizing."
Very simply, Bultmann believed that the gospels, like all good
stories, are built on the common mythology which underlies our
religious convictions. The first job was to isolate the myths, those
great stories which are so necessary to our identity and self-
understanding. For Bultmann the myth of the "dying and rising
gods" which was present in the ancient Mediterranean world
had its parallels in the passion and resurrection accounts of the
gospels. If the temporal clothing of the hero could be stripped
away, we would recognize the eternal truth which was present.
Then all we had to do was to reclothe the hero in contemporary
dress—"remythologizing." Unfortunately, the purpose and
technique of the demythologizing was never cleared up and the
remythologizing was almost completely forgotten.

This led some German scholars to propose a new hermeneutic
or system of interpretation based on the insight that the text
interprets the reader instead of vice versa. This also would have
closed the gap between then and now, but it too got lost in vague
intricacies and questionable philosophies about identity. At any
rate, the problem of interpreting for contemporary needs (which
is what I mean by hermeneutics) as distinct from simply explaining a text in its original context (which is usually called exegesis)
has been clear to the more astute historical critics. It is not a problem which is easily set aright and so it has often been ignored.

8. Conclusion

The scientific interpreter tries to leave nothing to chance, but in
the end faith supplies the certainties. This is the paradox of the sit-

uation. We want to be logical and scientific. In order to be so we must have theories and philosophies which are themselves based on faith. The traditional faith of Christendom also admitted that this was true. The medieval theologians accepted as a bedrock a "deposit of faith" on which they erected their science. If it was not more logical, it was at least more honest. By the time we get to doing our scientific or critical interpretations of the biblical texts we are already a dozen faith decisions at least down the path.

The *summa theologica*, the synthesis of all knowledge of theology, the "queen of the sciences" which the medieval teachers talked of, did manage to put all things in a somewhat reasonable order. Like everything else, in its heyday it went much too far. But the claim was relatively modest for all that. It organized our intellectual life and gave us an identity. We knew who we were and we could be right or wrong. We do not have that undergirding of realized faith today and so we suffer from the "who-am-I?" and "who-knows-what-is right-or-wrong?" syndrome. The next chapter will examine what seems to happen to us as individual interpreters.

ENDNOTES

1. Terrence J. Keegan, *Interpreting the Bible: A Popular Introduction to Biblical Hermeneutics* (New York: Paulist, 1985), 40–72, has probably as clear an explanation of this complex subject as one can find. Some structuralists, such as Polzin, have stated that if one understands a structuralist, one has misunderstood. The results sometimes appear to bear this out as the exotic vocabulary and meanings multiply.
2. Quoted by Richard Neuhaus in *Biblical Interpretation in Crisis: The Ratzinger Conference on Bible and Church* (Grand Rapids: Eerdmans, 1989), 114.
3. The term "historical Jesus" came into prominence with the famous book of Albert Schweitzer, *The Quest of the Historical Jesus*, published in 1906. Schweitzer's book spelled the end of the then liberal quest for reconstructing the historical figure of Jesus. Schweitzer pictured the real Jesus as a noble but deluded fanatic. The quest still goes on in many different directions, as the present publicity over the new historical Jesus indicates.

4. Nikos Kazantzakis, *The Last Temptation of Christ* (New York: Simon and Schuster, 1960), 477.

5. *Ratzinger Conference*, 114.

6. *Ratzinger Conference*, 119–122, "A Disputed Exegetical Establishment," brought out some fairly testy feelings that contemporary interpretation is dictated in university academia by the exegetical establishment of scholars, perhaps as represented by the American Academy of Religion. This is a shift from the church establishment which for many centuries dictated methods and conclusions.

7. George Lindbeck in *Ratzinger Conference*, 120.

6

The Interpreters of the Jesus Story

1. Who Was Paul?

A god who died for our sins: redemption through faith: resurrection after death—all these are counterfeits of true Christianity for which that disastrous wrong-headed fellow, Paul, must be held responsible.

F. Nietzsche

There has probably seldom been any one at the same time hated with such fiery hatred and loved with such strong passion as Paul.

A. Deissmann

In the scholastics I lost Christ but found him again in Paul.

M. Luther

I hold St. Paul to have been the first great corrupter of Christianity.

J.S. Mill

It was Paul who converted the religion that has raised one man above sin and death into a religion that delivered millions of men so completely into their dominion that their own common nature became a horror to them, and the religious life became a denial of life.

G.B. Shaw

The man who, I suppose, did more than anybody else to distort and subvert Christ's teaching was Paul.

A.N. Whitehead

No one understood Paul till Marcion, and he misunderstood him.

A. von Harnack

These accolades and condemnations[1] are symptomatic of how important Paul the interpreter has been for the acceptance or rejection of Christianity. Does the problem lie in the diversity of data which these authors had available? Was it in the methods that they used? Or was it in some personal criteria? Was a Resident Alien, as I have called it, operating as an interpreter within them? It was certainly not incompetence; all of the above were scholars of repute. Some prejudice and not a little arrogance may be detected, but that is probably not the answer. I could have quoted Adolf Hitler as an example of that: "Christ was an Aryan. But Paul used his teaching to mobilize the underworld and to organize an earlier Bolshevism." That is the face of ignorance and prejudice. What provoked such discordant responses? And how did Paul go about his interpreting?

2. *The Anonymous Story-Tellers Before Paul*

The one undoubted historical fact in biblical studies is that within twenty or twenty-five years after the death of Jesus, the first writer, Paul, was asserting both facts and interpretations about this Jesus. What do we know about the Jesus story before Paul and who was responsible for it?

It is generally accepted that before anything was written or collected there was an oral tradition. An oral tradition must belong to anonymous people in some way. Without their knowledge and interest in the story no audience or tradition survives. Moreover, when the oral tradition of the story first surfaces in the writing of Paul it is already interpretative. Any good story is interpretative since it has a point to make. The original people who accepted this story and handed it on to the next group were already interpreting.[2]

3. Paul as the Interpreter

In his earliest letters Paul simply takes it for granted that his readers already know and have given him information about the story of Jesus. He can compress his historical facts into a brief formula: "was crucified, was buried, was raised."[3] The only other biographical information about Jesus which he gives is that Jesus was "descended from David" (Rom 1:3; 2 Tim 2:8) and a reference in 1 Corinthians 7:10 to an instruction of the Lord about separation of wife from husband. Nothing is said in Paul of Jesus' birth, his family, his wondrous deeds, his sermons, the details of his passion or his physical activity after he was raised from the dead. Paul's letters clearly indicate that his readers knew much more about the Jesus story than his letters mention and that Paul himself had taught them about it before baptizing them. The Acts of the Apostles suggests that Paul did present a lengthy program of instruction for his catechumens, at least in Corinth and Ephesus.[4]

The Jesus story which Paul taught was at root historical. The clearest reference is in 1 Corinthians 15:1–8.[5] His readers have heard about the resurrection from eye-witnesses, some of whom are still alive. This leaves no doubt that Paul is talking of a person whom he and his readers considered real and historical. 1 Corinthians 15:14 draws the interpreted conclusion: "And if Christ has not been raised, then empty [too] is our preaching; empty, too, your faith." Paul is arguing here from facts and interpretations which the Corinthians already accepted.

Sometimes, indeed, he seems to have been dependent on his disciples for facts and interpretations. The eucharist, which Paul had not experienced personally at the last supper, is apparently already a ritual based on a tradition Paul received according to 1 Corinthians 11:23–26.[6] It is also interpreted as working salvation by the breaking of the body of Jesus and the pouring out of a new covenant in his blood.

Paul seems to refer to this Jesus story when he uses the word "gospel." In the whole possible set of Paul's writing the word is used fify-eight times.[7] So it is of some frequency. Whatever formal definition we may presume Paul had of the secular word "gospel," it necessarily included some news content. The basic meaning is some sort of announcement of an event. It is Paul's "gospel" only in the sense that he preached a version of it; it was "ours" as shared by his collaborators or readers; it was different from what some outside his circle were preaching (though we can't tell where the differences lie, whether in the narrative or in the interpretation). Paul's gospel was "a word of truth," "the mystery," which is an interpretative element.

Paul (and apparently the earlier Jesus story) begins his interpretation from the already accepted starting point of all the mythological stories—namely, the felt need for salvation. Paul shares with his readers often enough the remembrance of the sad state before his and their conversion. Indeed, in Romans 1:20–31 he paints a dreadful picture of the need for salvation which was experienced in the Roman world.[8]

Paralleling the classic myths, Paul pictures Jesus as the hero who was sent from the Father into the world to save it. Paul's basic facts, "was crucified," "was buried," "was raised," are almost always used in interpretative passages. The interpretation Paul puts on these expressions usually is that this ending of the story was a divinely decreed plan to save us and that it was the power of God which raised Jesus from the dead.

This is then applied to the individual Christian in the new vocation. It is the power of Jesus which has saved them, which has given them a hopeful and honorable present which they must live out, and which leads to a future where Jesus the savior has become the total ruler and encompassing head of all.

He is the image of the invisible God
    the firstborn of all creation.
For in him were created all things in heaven and on earth
    the visible and the invisible,
        whether thrones or dominions or principalities or powers;

all things were created through him and for him.
He is before all things,
    and in him all things hold together.
He is the head of the body, the church.
He is the beginning, the firstborn from the dead,
    that in all things he himself might be preeminent.
For in him all the fullness was pleased to dwell,
    and through him to reconcile all things for him,
    making peace by the blood of his cross (through him),
    whether those on earth or those in heaven.

Col 1:15–20

Not only is Paul interpreting; his argument presupposes that his hearers have already begun their own interpretation of the Jesus story in ways which he thinks needs correction.[9] Yet he has confidence that those who come after him will be faithful to the tradition which he has handed on to them. It is generally admitted that the pastoral epistles, which are in the spirit of Paul, stress the handing on of the tradition.[10]

In short, at the entry level to the historical Jesus in Paul we already have traditions which he has accepted as real and interpretations which he and his readers already know about. The rest of Paul is further interpretation of what the accepted facts are really saying.

4. Paul the Missionary

Paul was not a theoretician; he demanded commitment to the Savior story which he shared with his readers. An examination of the introductions to his letters, especially the earlier ones, indicates that Paul expected his readers to take some part in his own mission of spreading the gospel. The introductory thanksgivings often emphasize a sharing or cooperation in the spread of the gospel. In Philippians 1:3–11 Paul twice refers to the Philippians as "partners" in this work.[11] In the earlier epistles Paul uses "church" to refer to a local gathering of believers and implies that in some way they are conscious of and active in spreading the gospel. In the later epistles "church" has become the whole church which spreads beyond this world, and the missionary thrust is much more directed toward acting in accordance with the gospel.

A good illustration of how Paul was giving practical interpretation to the Jesus story in this way can be found in 1 Thessalonians. That epistle is the first of his letters, written about 51 B.E. If we read that brief letter through, or, even better, listen to it read publicly as the original audience heard it, we can understand how Paul linked hard historical facts, basic interpretations and demands for commitment. At the beginning he has a distinctively Jewish thanksgiving which covers the first half of the letter. What is he thanking them for? Mostly, he is thanking them for being with him in the new religion as missionaries: "We give thanks to God always for all of you, remembering you in our prayers, unceasingly calling to mind your work of faith and labor of love and endurance in hope of our Lord Jesus Christ, before our God and Father, knowing, brothers loved by God, how you were chosen" (1 Thes 1:2–4).

And so it goes as he recounts how much of a good example they are to others, how selflessly he worked among them and how much they responded, and then slowly how much they have both suffered for their new life. He worried about how they were doing and he has just welcomed back his co-laborer Timothy who had visited Thessalonica a second time and reassured him that these new Christians were persevering. At the end of the thanksgiving he prays that "the Lord make you increase and abound in love for one another and for all, just as we have for you" (1 Thes 3:12).

Now this is a very subtle way of persuading them to listen to what he will say in the second half of the letter, although he has already prepared them by some of the interpretations he has previously given them about the Jesus story. One cannot miss the commendations which are pleasing. However, commendations are never presented as accomplishments, neither his nor theirs, but as gifts. The gifts come from Jesus, but Jesus is not just an historical figure or a story character anymore; he is the Lord Jesus

Christ (1 Thes 1:3), a title which associates him with God and specifies him as one anointed for a mission. The "word" is the "word of the Lord" (1 Thes 1:8) or the "gospel of God" (1 Thes 2:2, 8, 13), even though it was Paul who was doing the instructing. This is Paul's first bold step into interpreting the meaning of the "gospel" which goes far beyond the physical facts.

The second part of the letter is an exhortation to make further progress in the faith, love and hope which he mentioned at the beginning (1 Thes 1:3). The Thessalonians are being tested by problems of daily living and especially by the expectation of some of the converts that the glorious return or *parousia* of Jesus is about to manifest itself again. They have given up responsible working for a living and they grieve for those who have already died in the brief time since Paul first came to them.

In addressing this problem Paul has recourse to reinterpreting his traditional understanding of the future life which he had as a Jew. That the world-story was going somewhere was a staple of Jewish belief. There was a "day" when God would make known how he had controlled history all along for his own glory. Sometimes "the day" was a threat, sometimes a consolation. Paul reinterpreted the tradition by making "Christ" the central figure in the victory.

My major interest here has been in the way in which Paul, our earliest writer, has used the existing data and interpretation of the Jesus story as paralleling the myths, all of which recognized the need for a savior God.

My second point relates to what Paul is saying as he goes beyond this interpretation. The story of the proclamation of the kingdom, the rejection of Jesus, and the humiliation of his death does not seem in itself to be very appealing. We would not consider it good PR. The interpretation of what was behind these brutal facts became the most important element. Whether Paul initiated these interpretations—certainly he did not do all of it—or whether he was the first to write them down—which, as far as we know, he did—we cannot say. But these first writings of a Christian do interpret Jesus as Lord, Christ, Son, Savior, Redeemer, etc. They come out of Paul's personal experience, but also out of his awareness of a communal tradition, his culture, his story-telling techniques and his growing maturity. Why should such preaching appeal?

The commonality of the theme in the myths and the common use of story-telling drawn from experience matched the hearers' understanding of their own maturing and ordering of their own lives at a critical moment. Paul's world was in a stage of crisis; the old stories no longer worked. Paul set off vital responses which his hearers were not even aware of until he uncovered them. He touched a nerve of need among those who heard the gospel. His Christian communities discovered a realistic Hero and a model for themselves.[12]

His constant appeals to the communities are not clever rhetorical tricks; they are his understanding of the deepest urges within us for identity. In identifying Jesus, Paul also identifies us. In his exhortations he calls Christians saints. He urges them to be aware of their dignity as children of God. This set off the whole chain of subsequent interpretation in the Christian community.

Paul was a genius. The interpretation of the Jesus story which he gives is filtered through himself—his personal experiences and his tradition. He has reinterpreted the tradition as had been done so often in the Israelite past, both the very ancient traditions of Judaism and the more recent tradition of the Jesus story. Paul had the genius to organize this to a large extent and to put the right word of persuasion on it. It appealed to something in his hearers which, by a long-buried instinct, they knew corresponded to their longings and needs. It also infuriated those who did not think they needed a savior.

5. The Gospels as Interpreters

The gospels which are much later than Paul rely on the same oral tradition.[13] They expand on the marvelous deeds, the sayings, the conflicts, and the actual course of Jesus' trial, death and resurrection which Paul took for granted that his readers already knew. But they are still interpreted data for specific communities. They still begin with the need for salvation which dominates the Old Testament and conforms to the mono-myth. This was what the readers of the four gospels had learned from experience, both personal and communal.

When Bultmann, the principal originator of our present historical criticism, began his study, he used proverbs as the base point.[14] Proverbs are folk sayings arising from common experience. Bultmann also posited that the evangelists understood the basic myths.[15] The essentials are a conviction of the need for salvation which is not obtainable by human industry or genius, the entry of a savior figure from outside, some sort of conflict and rejection ending in death and a handing on of the possibility of a new life. Bultmann realized that his contemporary culture did not have the same mythological stories as the original readers and that his readers were likely to miss the point hidden in the ancient tales. So he advocated that we must first "demythologize" the gospels (an unfortunate term). The ancient myths which he thought were the closest antecedents of the gospel stories were those of the "dying and rising gods" in existing Hellenistic culture. Then he tried to validate that there was a definite borrowing from these pagan stories. Thus there was a reasonable, human answer as to why people accepted Christianity.

However, Christianity still appeals and we do not need to borrow from the "dying and rising gods." That the Christian master-story fits into the mono-myth simply says that it fits human needs, not that it is borrowed. The race and its writers do not need to borrow what is already their own; they simply need the genius to detect its presence.

The story-telling was carried along in the gospels and in subsequent ages by the plot of the Jesus story and the character of Jesus. The character of Jesus as Son of God and universal savior is the most important interpretation of character. This was not mere academic theorizing but something learned by action. A homily from the second century says: "Brethren, we ought to regard Jesus Christ as God and judge of the living and the dead. We should not hold our savior in low esteem, for if we esteem him but little, we may hope to obtain but little from him. Moreover, people who hear these things and think of them of small importance commit sin, and we ourselves sin if we do not realize what we have been called from, who has called us, and to what place, and how much suffering Jesus Christ endured on our account."[16] Not only is the teaching perfectly Pauline; it also relies on the same approach beginning with experience and it reaches the same conclusion that salvation has come to us in crisis through Jesus Christ. It is also noteworthy that the source is anonymous; it was spoken not by some great theologian of the church, but the ordinary belief of an ordinary preacher and an ordinary congregation. The mono-myth of salvation is assuming its Christian form.

Whatever early Christianity did, it gave identity to a people. This is what the great mythic stories always do. Incidentally, it destroyed the myths of the surrounding culture. It did not destroy mythology; it replaced it with one which was paradoxically both more transcendent and more practical. The desire to become like God became more transparent in the historical hero, Jesus. Yet in the traditional cry of Julian the Apostate, "Galilean, thou hast conquered," we do not have the surrender of an emperor or the confession of a philosopher; we have a moralist admitting that he was overcome by a more practical ethics.

However, unlike myth strictly so-called, this master story with its plot of salvation is anchored in basic historical facts. Even the most unbelieving liberal historian accepts the historical facts of the beginning and diffusion of Christianity at a definable point in time. John Meier, a Catholic, in his *New York Times* book review "Jesus Among the Historians," ends up by appealing to this argument.[17] The belief of the earliest Christian church is affirmed as historical despite the divergences of details in the four canonized gospels; the ancient authors and readers could see the divergences as well as we can. The story-line overshadowed the historical details by giving them a meaning, and sometimes the meaning even created minor details. For an historian of facts this would be disastrous; for a story-teller it simply added richness to the telling.

6. Summing Up

No one has yet put a finger on the center of Paul's interpretation of the Jesus story in a definitive manner. It is admitted that it is decisive for understanding why Christianity has its appeal or its rejection. We may, however, list some of the basic points in Paul's approach.

1. Paul took for granted that his readers acknowledged that they had a need for salvation from present woes for which they were in some way responsible. He says so explicitly in Romans 3:10. It is a presupposition both from the Old Testament background and from the general myths of the human race.
2. He and his readers took for granted that an historical nucleus of the Jesus story was indisputable. Paul had his own personal conversion experience and presumed that his readers had something similar. Beyond that he accepted much of the Jesus story from what he was told by others. Within that story were already the basic interpretations which Paul would develop and which Christians would accept. Jesus was already called "Lord" and "savior" by the time Paul began to write.
3. The acceptance of the Jesus story carried with it a commitment to live according to the "handed down" interpretation. Individuals and the community were to accept that their lives, present and future, would be like that of Jesus. They were not only seeking "the good life"; they were also missionaries by the way that they lived.
4. The community was bonded together by an identity as the "body of Christ." They were a holy or separate group not just as a group in society which could be named; they were part of a mysterious union which was headed by the other-worldly, cosmic Son of God who made us children of God also. This was a hope that the common mythology had always striven for but had never dared to say. The Jesus story would end with a final revelation that this had been happening throughout our history.

ENDNOTES

1. Malcolm Muggeridge, *Paul, Envoy Extraordinary* (New York: Harper & Row, 1972), 11–16 has collected a large sampling of quotes from which these are chosen.
2. Frank Beare, *The Earliest Records of Jesus* (New York: Abingdon, 1962), "The Making of the Synoptic Gospels and Their Relationship to One Another," 13–16, and "Factors in the Transmission of the Tradition concerning Jesus," 16–22, has a fair summary of the normal conclusions.
3. This triple description is used in the following passages:
    crucified—1 Cor 1:13, 23; 2:2, 8; 2 Cor 13:3; Gal 3:1; 6:14. Rom 6:6 asserts: "We know that our old self was crucified with him," which is, of course, an interpretation which does presume the real crucifixion of Jesus.
    died—Rom 5:6, 8; 6:10; 8:34; 14:9, 15; 1 Cor 8:11; 15:3; 2 Cor 5:14, 15; Gal 2:21; 1 Thes 4:14.
    rose—1 Thes 4:14.
    was raised—Rom 6:4; 7:4; 8:34; 14:9 ("came to life"); 1 Cor 15:4; 2 Cor 5:15.
4. Acts 18:1–18a tells the story of Paul's term of teaching in Corinth: "He settled there for a year and a half and taught the word of God among them." Acts 19:1–20:1 has a more formal setting for the teaching in Ephesus. "He withdrew and took his disciples with him and began to hold daily discussions in the lecture hall of Tyrannus. This continued for two years with the result that the inhabitants of the province of Asia heard the word of the Lord, Jews and Greeks alike."
5. 1 Cor 15:1–8: "Now I am reminding you, brothers, of the gospel I preached to you, which you indeed received and in which you also stand. Through it you are also being saved, if you hold fast to the word I preached to you, unless you believed in vain. For I handed on to you as of first importance what I also received: that Christ died for our sins in accordance with the scriptures; that he was buried; that he was raised on the third day in accordance with the scriptures; that he appeared to Cephas, then to the twelve. After that, he appeared to more than five hundred brothers at once, most of whom are still living, though some have fallen asleep. After that he appeared to James, then to all the apostles. Last of all, as to one born abnormally, he appeared to me."
6. 1 Cor 11:23–26: "For I received from the Lord what I also handed on to you, that the Lord Jesus, on the night he was handed over, took bread,

and after he had given thanks, broke it and said, 'This is my body that is for you. Do this in remembrance of me.' In the same way also the cup, after supper, saying, 'This cup is the new covenant in my blood. Do this, as often as you drink it, in remembrance of me.' For as often as you eat this bread and drink the cup, you proclaim the death of the Lord until he comes."

7. Paul's use of "gospel" is broad and varied.

   a. "the gospel" by itself in Rom 1:15, 16; 11:28; 15:20; 1 Cor 1:17; 4:15; 9:14, 16, 18, 23; 2 Cor 8:18; 10:16; Gal 2:2, 5, 7, 14; 4:13; Eph 3:6; 6:19; Phil 1:5, 7, 12, 16, 27; 2:22; 4:3, 15; Col 1:5; 1 Thes 2:4; 2 Tim 1:8, 10; Phm 1:13. Total—31 times. No pattern seems to exist here.

   b. "Gospel" is modified as:

      1) "the gospel of God"—Rom 1:1; 15:16; 2 Cor 11:7; 1 Thes 2:8, 9; 1 Tim 1:11 ("the glorious gospel of the blessed God")

      2) "the gospel of (or about) Christ (or Son)—Rom 1:3, 9; 15:19; 1 Cor 9:12; 2 Cor 2:12; 9:13; 10:14; 1 Thes 2:18; 3:2 (the gospel of our Lord Jesus). No significant pattern emerges for me in these variations.

      3) "my gospel"—Rom 2:16; 16:25; 2 Tim 1:10. 1 Cor 15:1 has: "Now I am reminding you, brothers, of the gospel I preached to you, which you indeed received and in which you also stand." "Our gospel": 2 Cor 4:3; 1 Thes 1:5; 2 Thes 2:14.

      4) other modifiers: "our gospel is veiled"—2 Cor 4:3; "The light of the gospel of the glory of Christ, who is the image of God"—2 Cor 4:4; "a different gospel"—2 Cor 11:4; Gal 1:6; "a gospel other than the one that we preached to you"— 1:8; "a gospel other than the one you received"—1:9; "the mystery of the gospel"—Eph 6:19; "your partnership for the gospel"— Phil 1:15; "the word of truth, the gospel"—Col 1:5. Now I am not looking for a word pattern in such a vocabulary study, but for an historical implication about the Jesus story.

8. Obviously on such a crucial point we have many denials and explanations which make the spread of Christianity reasonable. Some argue that conditions in the Roman empire of the time were quite tolerable. Peace and a modest livelihood were available to most. So there was no great desire for salvation. The denunciations of Roman writers of their own society are dismissed as exceptional. However, Paul and his readers were aware of a deeper yearning for personal and communal salvation than the sociological or political circumstances which contemporary critics want to make the criterion.

9. Rom 10:14: "But how can they call on him in whom they have not

believed? And how can they believe in him of whom they have not heard? And how can they hear without someone to preach?" Rom 10:16: "But not everyone has heeded the good news; for Isaiah says, 'Lord, who has believed what was heard from us?'" Rom 10:17: "Thus faith comes from what is heard, and what is heard comes through the word of Christ." Gal 1:12: "For I did not receive it from a human being, nor was I taught it, but it came through a revelation of Jesus Christ." Eph 1:13: "In him you also, who have heard the word of truth, the gospel of your salvation, and have believed in him, were sealed with the promised Holy Spirit." Eph 4:21: "assuming that you have heard of him and were taught in him, as truth is in Jesus." Col 1:5: "because of the hope reserved for you in heaven. Of this you have already heard through the word of truth, the gospel." Col 1:6: "that has come to you, just as in the whole world it is bearing fruit and growing, so also among you, from the day you heard it and came to know the grace of God in truth." Col 1:23: "provided that you persevere in the faith, firmly grounded, stable, and yet not shifting from the hope of the gospel that you have heard, which has been preached to every creature under heaven, of which I, Paul, am a minister. Col 2:7: "rooted in him and built upon him and established in the faith as you were taught, abounding in thanksgiving."

10. 2 Tim 3:14–17: "But you, remain faithful to what you have learned and believed, because you know from whom you learned it, and that from infancy you have known [the] sacred scriptures, which are capable of giving you wisdom for salvation through faith in Christ Jesus. All scripture is inspired by God and is useful for teaching, for refutation, for correction, and for training in righteousness, so that one who belongs to God may be competent, equipped for every good work."

11. Especially significant for this "partnership" in preaching the gospel are the thanksgivings found mostly at the beginnings of the epistles. Philippians 1:3–7 is the clearest statement: "I give thanks to my God at every remembrance of you, praying always with joy in my every prayer for all of you, because of your partnership for the gospel from the first day until now. I am confident of this, that the one who began a good work in you will continue to complete it until the day of Christ Jesus. It is right that I should think this way about all of you, because I hold you in my heart, you who are all partners with me in grace, both in my imprisonment and in the defense and confirmation of the gospel." 1 Thes 1:5–8: "For from you the word of the Lord has sounded forth not only in Macedonia and Achaia, but in every place

your faith in God has gone forth, so that we have no need to say anything." 1 Cor 1:7: "so that you are not lacking in any spiritual gift as you wait for the revelation of our Lord Jesus Christ." In the list of spiritual gifts in 1 Cor 12 the emphasis is always on gifts which concern preaching the gospel. 2 Cor 1:3–11 is a thanksgiving for the help of their prayers in Paul's work of preaching the gospel. Rom 1:3–15 is a long thanksgiving which centers on the shared faith and spiritual gifts. At the end Paul enlists their practical aid for his coming mission to Spain.

In the early epistles Paul uses "church" to mean a local community whose partnership he seeks and exhorts them to preach the gospel either by going out to surrounding areas or by living exemplary lives. In the captivity letters "church" has become universalized and the references to actual preaching are downplayed. The exemplar function of witnessing to the gospel, however, remains in the ethical instructions.

Eduard Schweizer, "The Church as the Missionary Body of Christ," *NTS* 8 (1961–62), 1–11, analyzes Romans from the viewpoint of salvation for the whole race (not just individual conversions). For Schweizer, Paul visualizes a total involvement of the Christian group in spreading the gospel by preaching and ethical actions.

12. A numerical survey of the titles used for Christ reveals some preliminary notions. *Christ* (i.e., the anointed one) is used alone some 193 times. The composite *Jesus Christ* which uses his personal name occurs some 91 times. The solemn *Lord Jesus Christ* occurs 62 times. *Lord Jesus* is used 22 times. It is notable that "Lord Jesus" seems to be the favorite expression in the Thessalonian correspondence where "Lord Jesus Christ" is never used. *Jesus* alone is used only 11 times. Oddly, it is not used in 1 Cor 15:1–11 where Paul is talking about the historical Jesus. In general, Paul is not greatly interested in the human "Jesus"—what he did, what he said, etc., except in his crucifixion and resurrection. His central interest is in "Jesus Christ" (the Messiah). The divine Jesus is at least hinted at in "Lord Jesus Christ"; most of those uses, however, are found in the more formal introductions/thanksgivings at the beginning of the letters and in the final greetings at the end. Christ is also called "Son of God," "the Father's Son," "his own Son." Paul probably adopted these titles and designations from the Jesus story which preceded him. Jesus is the savior, the redeemer, and, in the later epistles, the *icon* or image of God, the *pleroma* or fullness, etc.

13. What I am talking about is not sources. If we talk about Q or Proto-

Mk, or M or L, we are not talking about authoritative persons, but about popular traditions whatever they may be. When Matthew, Mark, Luke, and John were finally attached to the works as titles, they remained anonymous. Whatever authority they may now have comes from later traditions or scholarly pursuits. We have become used to "The School of Matthew," "The Johannine Community," "The Community of Matthew," etc., all of which describe popular groups. At first they were simply oral traditions of some believers. Nor if we posit a time when they began to be written down can we attach authoritative names to the first writers.

14. Rudolf Bultmann, *The History of the Synoptic Tradition* (New York: Harper & Row, 1963), 14. "The Tradition of the Sayings of Jesus" begins with that odd word "apophthegm" by which he means popular sayings: "It also seems to me a secondary matter whether one begins with sayings or stories. I start with sayings. But I should reckon as part of the tradition of the sayings a species of traditional material which might well be reckoned as stories—viz. such as units of sayings set in a brief context." "I shall proceed first by analyzing the particular instances of a species of apophthegm individually and then go on to discuss their form-history in a brief review" (11). His next major division is "Dominical Sayings" which first treats "Logia (Jesus as the Teacher of Wisdom)." In both cases he is dealing with sayings of the people or sayings which were accepted by the people. These are not pronouncements from an authority, such as the later use of prophetic quotes from the Old Testament.

15. Bultmann's ideas on myth are neither very clear nor convincing. Cf. Hans Werner Bartsch, *Kerygma and Myth: A Theological Debate by Rudolf Bultmann* (New York: Harper & Row, 1961). Joseph Campbell does better on the details but has even less concern for historical foundation. Cf. Joseph Campbell, *The Hero with a Thousand Faces* (New York: Pantheon, 1949) and *The Power of Myth* (New York: Doubleday, 1988).

16. Reading for the 32nd Sunday in Ordinary Time, in *Prayer of Christians* (New York: Catholic Book Publishing Co., 1975).

17. John P. Meier, "Jesus Among the Historians," (*New York Times* book review, Dec. 21, 1986). This is an ancient argument. St. John Chrysostom in a homily on 1 Corinthians 4:3–4 uses the same argument. See The Liturgy of the Hours, Reading for the Feast of St. Bartholomew, August 24.

7

The History of the Resident Alien

1. Retelling the Story

In the beginning the Timeless sent a beam of power which traveled through the universe and touched a small planet. A child was born. As it toddled about it looked with wide-eyed wonder at all things, and as children will, it gave them a name. The names were wonderfully apt. Every day as the child grew it found more wondrous things and it wanted to name and understand them all. One day when the child had grown it came into a clearing in the forest. In the center were two stones, completely unmarked and of an unknown kind. When the youth looked at one he felt within himself such a surge of understanding and wisdom as he had never felt before; he not only knew endlessly more but he understood the connections and the reasons. When he looked at the other stone he felt such an upsurge of joyful life that he seemed to be on fire with it. One thing more he learned: he must never look at these stones again. Yet he was left with such an increase of understanding that now it made him sad. Although he could name all the things he saw and understand their purpose, he could not say: "And that is like me."

One day the power went out again from the Timeless and touched him and he saw Another. He was not alone. As the youth and the girl found delight in their world, they came one day upon a Man who was odd in appearance, even dressed in a suit and tie and with a beard. He said:

"Pleased to meet you; I am Doctor Young." Then he asked: "Have you studied all these things?" When they said that they had, he asked again: "Have you found the two stones?" "Yes," they said, "but we were told never to look at them again." "Ah, me," said the Doctor. "My assistants are sometimes overzealous. Actually, the stones belong to my university; only those who have a doctorate and life-time tenure are allowed to view them. However," he said, "if you care to enroll now, I might make an exception." "What are the stones?" they asked. "As you experienced," the Doctor said, "they give you the fullness of life and knowledge (and then he smiled humbly and bowed) like myself." "Then you made all of this yourself," they exclaimed. "Yes," he said, "and rather well, too. In some circles they call me God rather than Doctor." And so they were enrolled and led to see the two stones.

The two of them suddenly became conscious that they were not dressed in clothes as the Doctor was and they fled into the forest. Then they saw another One and they knew that he was the Father. He was walking through the forest slowly and delightedly examining everything he saw. "Where are you?" he said. "We're in the forest," they said. "Why are you there?" "We are naked and are ashamed," they said. "Who told you to be ashamed?" he asked. "Doctor Young," they said and the Father responded, "Ah, yes, I thought so." Suddenly they saw Doctor Young but he was as naked as they were and not nearly so attractive. The Father said: "You are cursed, Doctor Young. You are the one who will learn something from these young ones. And you two," he added, "you will find out what life and wisdom are all about in the future after you have children. It will not be easy. But first," he added, "we must make you some clothes." So the Father sat down, folded his legs like a tailor and carefully began to make some exquisite clothes. When he fitted them with their clothes, they did bear a resemblance to him. After that he took them by the hand and led them to a high iron fence and a great gate. Outside the gate was a thicket not at all like the pleasant garden-like forest they had known. "Out you go," he said, "until you have learned enough to come back." And so he closed the gate and set two MPs there. They presented arms while he checked off some invisible flaws in their dress and handed them mysterious batons like flashlights. "Here now," he said. "You watch those two. They will try to get back any way they can, but you keep them out until I tell you to let them in." With that the Father walked away to continue his stroll in the garden.

I apologize for this incompetent retelling of the garden of Eden story. I do not apologize for attempting to retell the ancient story in somewhat contemporary terms. That, after all, is what the author of Genesis did. Fortunately, he understood much better than I how to tell a story well and how to make it truly relevant.

2. Interpretation and Reinterpretation

The previous chapter examined how Paul interpreted the Jesus story which preceded him. Much of it was re-interpretation from an Old Testament background and from the necessary myths of the race. Such reinterpretation for contemporary needs has been called hermeneutics.[1] Unfortunately contemporary scholars tend to shy away from it and talk of it only in terms of principles and methods. It would be more honest as well as more effective to start with the experience of reinterpretation which our faith community has had.

The Old Testament is much more a record of "reinterpretation" of events, stories and sayings from the past than any kind of on-the-spot report. For example, all the stories of Genesis are theological interpretations of events that had happened long before. The account was written much later, somewhere between the tenth and fifth centuries B.C.E. Faithful Jews tried to reinterpret the ancient mythological traditions and legends of their heroes from their own traditions for the contemporary needs of their co-religionists. The seven days of creation is a magnificent adaptation of fairly common stories of creation. It seems to have been written in a time of despair at the lowest point of adherence to, or confidence in, Israel's belief in Yahweh, their God. In the time of the Babylonian captivity a great dramatist reinterpreted the story to make the point that everything was beautiful and in order, that men and women were made in the image and likeness of God, and that God had now done his work and was resting while his people took care of the world.

Even the so-called historical books, such as the Deuteronomist's history (the books of Samuel and Kings), selectively pick out incidents which will serve the needs of the people; for the actual records one is referred to the royal archives. This is reflective writing; the Deuteronomist's history ends at 2 Kings 25:27–30 with a mystery, and that is surely a proper interpretation of their contemporary life. Walter Bruggemann has popularized the idea that the psalms represent three stages of faith; first an old statement of religious belief, then the doubts, and finally the reintegration of the belief into a much more mature theology.[2]

In a similar way Christian scriptures began to be interpreted as soon as (or sooner than) they were accepted. As noted in the previous chapter about 1 Thessalonians, Paul was the first great interpreter of the Jesus story. He has little to say of what Jesus actually did; he has much to say about how to interpret the gospel, "my gospel," for deep insight and practical use. The New Testament as a whole is largely interpretations of Jesus and often reinterpretations of an older version. The four gospels are not primarily factual reports of the deeds and sayings of Jesus. They have that quality at times, but they were much more reports of what four individual Christian communities accepted as the basic spiritual interpretation of those deeds and sayings. The four gospels are full of divergences with one another, and that was perfectly obvious to the later gospel writers who composed them. Matthew's gospel does not make the same point as Mark's, and the synoptics are not at all like John. The disagreement did not bother the evangelists since the basic historical facts were already accepted.

3. Patristic Era

When the next generation of post-New Testament Christian writers began their work, they too reinterpreted the message anew for their time.[3] However, they did it from their own cultural background and needs which were different from the earlier writers and readers who came from a Jewish background. Among the earliest of those writers was Clement of Rome, reputedly a pope, who wrote somewhere between 70 and 100 C.E. In a long letter to the Corinthians, who were continuing their disputes, he cites Old Testament texts profusely. However, his attitude toward them is not that of a Hebrew wise man who savors their thoughts, but of a practical Roman who knows what may appeal to his audience. When he gets around to the nub of his instruction, he becomes the real Roman who uses military metaphors to tell the young dissidents that they are obliged to obey the elders as soldiers do their commanders.[4]

Ignatius of Antioch in Syria about 120 C.E. left nine letters while he was being transported to Rome for martyrdom. Clement had been concerned about giving specific orders to the church of Corinth; Ignatius was concerned about church order in general, especially hierarchy, in his area of influence. Ignatius was not a native Jew but apparently a Hellenist. He understood the need for organizational structure; he reinterpreted the vague references to church structure of the previous writings to a very definite system of bishops-deacons-priests as a court of teaching and dramatizing the doctrine in liturgy. It met the need of his time and place and eventually became the standard for the Church which he called "Catholic."

Meanwhile a converted lawyer in Rome was writing to defend his new-found faith especially against the Jews. Justin Martyr was well educated in the legal rhetoric of his time. He is factual, as a lawyer should be, and from him we learn some of the actual practices of the early Roman Church, such as the Sunday celebrations of the eucharist. He was also a philosopher, and his thought moves along those lines of logic which appealed to people of his time and social class.

As the Catholic Church spread and became richer in resources of both talent and money, "catechetical schools" were established to train new missionaries. Those at Alexandria and Antioch were the principal ones. Both represent the eastern side of the Mediterranean world. Although Alexandria is associated with a symbolic method of interpretation and Antioch with a literal method, the difference is not as great as the similarities.[5] Both were dependent on a common understanding that all the materials fitted together in some way. For example, the *Epistle of Barnabas*, which seems to come from the early second century and is in the Alexandrian tradition, makes a practical point of the story in Genesis that Abraham circumcised three hundred and eighteen of his household.[6] Three hundred and eighteen in Greek numbering is expressed by the letters *iota/epsilon* plus *tau*. The first two letters are the beginning of the name of Jesus and the last is a cross. So the writer concluded that the text refers to Jesus and has a Christian meaning. Now this may seem like legerdemain to us, and so do all of these odd numerical interpretations, but we have seen previously that sometimes they work. Those who accept them are convinced that they know the overall plan even though we think that they have reached into the wrong parts bin.

4. The Philosophers' Approach

As time went on the philosophical background of the fathers dominated the interpretative process. Their philosophy at least gave an assurance that they had an overall pattern of the universe which allowed them to define Christian dogmas more precisely. The great Christological and Trinitarian definitions of the fourth century came out of this ability to think in abstract terms. Jesus was a true human being and also truly divine in all ways, two natures in one person. One God alone exists but there are three persons in God. Jesus is Son of God but also son of Mary, and Mary is truly the mother of God, as the famous title *Theotokos* (God-maker) says. Such interpretations appealed to the mentality of the times and had enormous social and political importance.

Something similar happened with the ethical interpretation of the Christian code. For example, the Roman concern for law was an admirable thing, and the construction of whole codes of law logically arranged was an enormous advantage. It was not, however, the way the original semitic authors thought. When the New Testament was translated into Latin the legal viewpoint of Rome started to creep in. In 1 Corinthians 7:6 Paul, speaking in the tradition of Jewish wisdom, suggested that Christians might abstain from marital intercourse for the purpose of praying, but only for a time. His sentiment read literally: "This I say as a suggestion, not as a command." The Latin translated it: "This I say by way of indulgence..." which got translated later into English as "concession." The semitic mind had no idea of suggesting that marital intercourse was in any way indecent. But the Latin suggested that one needed some sort of excuse or permission to enjoy sex. In the fourth century Augustine, speaking from a prevailing Platonic mentality that the soul was imprisoned in an inferior body, and by his own unfortunate personal experience, thought that sex was bad. It was permitted only as an escape valve. The social conditions influenced interpretation.

And, vice versa, the moral teaching of the fathers influenced Christians in their social life at least to a certain extent.[7] Much of the writings of the fathers are sermons which they preached, and they are usually very practical although they never stray far from the basic doctrines. St. Peter Chrysologus (380–450) has a great sermon on what we would now call "self-image," but it is far more than that. "Why then, man, are you so worthless in your own eyes and yet so precious to God? Why render yourself such dishonor when you are honored by him? Why do you ask how you were created and do not seek to know why you were made? Was not this entire visible universe made for your dwelling? It was for you that the light dispelled the overshadowing gloom; for your sake was the night regulated and the day measured, and for you were the heavens embellished with the varying brilliance of the sun, the moon and the stars. The earth was adorned with flowers, groves and fruit; and the constant marvelous variety of lovely things was created in the air, the fields, and the seas for you, lest sad solitude destroy the joy of God's new creation. And the Creator still works to devise things that can add to your glory. He has made you in his image that you might in your person make the invisible Creator present on earth."[8]

5. The Medieval Interpreters

The conquest of Rome by the barbarians at the end of the fifth century destroyed the world-view which had been the basis on which society operated. For centuries, as Europe went into a decline, preservation of the writings of the fathers was a high concern.[9] Monks laboriously copied out the scriptures and the writings of the fathers, although they did not understand very deeply how the frequent moral exhortations applied and they certainly did not add much that was new. In some places such as Northumbria, England, in the eighth century Bede and Alcuin were truly scholars with an extensive library available and began to make some new contributions to interpretation. However, it was only in the flowering of the medieval ages, especially in the thirteenth century, that European Christianity regained an overall view of human affairs. Albert the Great and Thomas Aquinas were the culmination of a movement which once again erected a theoretical structure of the world into which all knowledge could be codified. These scholars were realists in their work, even in their concern for the accuracy of the biblical texts they were using. Enormous effort went into correcting the manuscripts, but the art and the artifacts were not sufficient to complete the enterprise. The great scholars were also aware of the need for precise literal meanings in the sacred scriptures before they began their theological interpretations. One had to study scripture before theology.

The realism and orderliness sought for in the scholarly world of the times reflected the social world of order in which everyone had a place. It worked to a certain extent; it was useful interpretation and it was expressed in useful ways. The great cathedrals of Europe and the universities were the symbols of the achievement.

6. Renaissance and Reformation

The Renaissance rediscovered the ancient culture of Greece and Rome on more visible and controllable lines, especially as ancient biblical texts from the eastern Mediterranean were discovered. More importantly the Renaissance renewed the ideal of the human being as the center of the universe. During the Reformation, scripture interpretation flowed much more from individual faith rather than from traditions of the fathers or church authority. Luther and Calvin were especially important in this change. The Renaissance brought out more fully the importance of the physical sciences which the medieval universities had begun to investigate. Slowly this led to the industrial revolution.

In actuality the reformers did not agree very much on how to interpret scripture and indeed encouraged a political system which was also very divisible. It is curious, then, that by the nineteenth century mainline Protestant interpretation had somewhat reversed itself, at least by becoming more literal and impersonal. The common focus seems slowly to have shifted to scientific historiography, and the late nineteenth and early twentieth centuries were dominated by historical criticism among Protestants. The highly visual nature of archeological discoveries did much to push this along. The organizing point for any faith or agnosticism, indeed for any synthesis, became simply the consensus of scholars on any particular point. Walter Lippmann in the days of Eisenhower once talked of the academic-military-industrial complex as the new papacy. The great problem among contemporary Protestants is to define something which makes the scriptures truly normative regardless of individual opinion.[10]

7. The Catholic Phenomenon

After and perhaps because of the reformation, Catholics more and more looked to hierarchy and scholars for their normative interpretation. The Council of Trent was largely a juridic approach to correcting practical abuses especially among the clergy. The hierarchy became the police and the scholars defined more exactly what was and was not proper conduct. They led the pack more than listened to the faithful. Rules and bureaucracies multiplied both in the hierarchy and in academia. The faithful were no longer the prime custodians of the Christian story, but the listeners. The wider vision of the church as a whole was obscured. When Vatican I defined the doctrine of infallibility of the pope in 1870, this was only the first item on the agenda. Due to political disturbances the fathers never got around to the rest of it, which concerned the bishops and laity. Unfortunately in the next century the "church" came to mean largely the hierarchy and the scholars. Even in such mundane things as publishing, before Vatican II a clear distinction was made between scholarly books and pious books. Obviously there was a pejorative connotation here. Pious devotions flourished but did not seem to enter deeply into the teaching decisions of hierarchy or academics nor into an integrated view of church and life.

The first reaction of Catholic academics to the new historical criticism was one of repudiation. In truth, the historicists were often rationalistic to such a point that they denied any inbreaking of the supernatural, such as miracles. To the scientific mind miracles were an absurdity. Catholic apologists in response tried to elevate physical miracles to divine proofs. The teaching element of the miracle stories was largely forgotten. Toward the end of the period, from 1905 to 1915, the Pontifical Biblical Commission issued a great number of decrees which effectively banned any serious discussion in print of the historical approach.

8. Post-Vatican II Developments

For Catholic biblical scholars the break-through came with the encyclical of Pius XII called *Divino Afflante Spiritu* in 1943. It validated the historical approach as legitimate and encouraged Catholic scholars to begin a new era of interpretation. The delay, at least, allowed Catholic scholarship to avoid some of the extremes of historicism into which others had fallen.

Vatican II gave an even greater spur to the people's interpretation. In its vision of the church the pilgrim people came first, then the hierarchy, and finally the scholars who were only mentioned incidentally. The practical result was to encourage bible study among the faithful. The reading of the bible had become almost a mark of the true Protestant instead of the true Catholic. Popular publications for Catholics began from Paulist Press, The Liturgical Press, the first Jerome Biblical Commentary and then a host of others.

The result has not been uniform nor entirely happy. George Lindbeck commented that Catholics as a whole have not become notable bible readers since Vatican II.[11] The result has been sporadic although real. At first it was thought that bible discussion groups could succeed only if there was a priest present; then we substituted a Catholic layperson with appropriate academic qualifications, and we now have ecumenical groups of lay persons. What has not yet emerged is some overall vision of church which directs all this discussion. We have not yet learned how to listen effectively to one another from top to bottom. "Base communities" have claimed more success but that too is spotty. It is not really a question of authority. It is rather a problem of the broader vision of the church; we still have too many single issue discussions going on.

These recent developments in Roman Catholic interpretation do highlight both the tradition and the contemporary usefulness. And so we are again caught between the need for some stabilized interpretation which is normative and for personal, spiritual meaning. We reach for "tradition," especially in the fathers or Thomistic theology or official statements, and yet we know that our responsibility must include a need for flexibility as we respond to the personal influence of the Holy Spirit.[12]

9. Conclusions

This admittedly Disneyland tour of two thousand years of complex history can certainly be both validated and questioned in details.[13] But two factors, important for our questioning, emerge. First, the quest for making the scriptures useful in every age and condition goes on relentlessly despite changes in society or in the academic theories of scholars. If the scriptures are not useful, they are not scriptures. If the interpretation is not useful, it is not accepted by the people. Yet we cannot simply be victims of social change, embracing each new enthusiasm or social movement. Hence the ceaseless ebb and flow of methods. The Catholic Church has never officially installed any one method as the authoritative one. Nor has the Catholic Church authoritatively defined the meaning of many specific texts. Among the thousands of verses in the bible less than twenty-five are involved in dogmatic decisions. None of the moral teachings is similarly defined. Yet these are the cutting edge of what it means to be a Catholic. The bishops' conference of the United States has issued courageous and astute pastoral letters on nuclear war and the economic system. These are not definitive statements but certainly reflect a trend in the thinking of many committed Catholics. They form part of the *sensus fidelium* —but not all of it.

Second, we are always looking for some master plan, some final explanation, some synthesis or *summa theologica* to help us use the parts of the sacred books as the whole church would have us do. Historical criticism is fading. So is our national confidence in science to manage either war or peace. In *The Ratzinger Conference* Cardinal Ratzinger insisted that we must find some new approach which goes beyond our present scholarly methods. George Lindbeck answered to the satisfaction of most of the participants by urging a return to the classic hermeneutic. That is what we must next consider.

ENDNOTES

1. Webster's Third International Dictionary (1961) defines hermeneutic as: "the study of the methodological principles of interpretation and explanation; specifically the study of the general principles of biblical interpretation."
2. Walter Brueggemann, *The Message of the Psalms* (Minneapolis: Augsburg, 1984), lists the steps as psalms of orientation, psalms of disorientation and psalms of new orientation.

3. Joseph W. Trigg, *Biblical Interpretation* (Wilmington: Glazier, 1988). Trigg notes that all the significant Greek and Latin fathers received a Hellenistic education. This centered on rhetoric, especially study of the classics such as Homer and Hesiod. The usual method was to find some symbolic meaning to make these readings contemporary. Mythology was properly understood. So it is not surprising that both Alexandria and Antioch were largely symbolic in their approach. They looked for typology. What unites the fathers is "style." "However sophisticated hermeneutically the fathers were, they could not conceive of interpreting the bible in any way divorced from the needs of the Christian community" (49).

4. The office, date and ethnic origin of Clement are all disputed. He certainly wrote with authority from Rome, but the claim that he was the third pope in our sense of that title is not dominant any longer. R. Brown and many others date the letter to about 100 C.E., J.A.T. Robinson to about 70 C.E. Most commentators incline to the opinion that Clement was a Gentile and see in his writing the growing influence of imperial Roman practice. The crucial paragraph of the letter states: "Let us, then, brethren, do soldiers' duty in downright earnest under the banner of his glorious commands." James A. Kleist, *The Epistles of St. Clement of Rome and St. Ignatius of Antioch* (Westminster: Newman, 1946), 32, paragraph 37.

5. Cyprian of Carthage (circa 200–258 C.E.) remarks in a treatise on the petition "Give us this day our daily bread" of the Lord's Prayer: "We can understand this petition in a spiritual and in a literal sense. For in the divine plan both senses may help toward our salvation." (Saint Cyprian, bishop and martyr, "Treatise on the Lord's Prayer," quoted in *The Liturgy of the Hours* [New York: Catholic Book Publishing Co., 1975], 11th week in Ordinary Time, Thursday.) Cyprian clearly knows about methods as well as we do and avoided the danger of making an exclusive choice of one. At the same time, he was firmly rooted to a pragmatic interpretation.

6. Trigg, *Biblical Interpretation*, 18.

7. Francis X. Murphy, *Politics and the Early Christian* (New York: Desclée, 1967) remarks in his epilogue that "The first four hundred years of the Christian experiment in dealing with the political organization of human life indicate clearly that in the civil sphere, at least, Christianity was not intended as a directly revolutionary force....Nor has the Christian had much greater success in injecting justice and right reason into the conduct of political affairs than the people of previous or other religious or secular dispensations" (167–168).

8. From a sermon for the feast of St. Peter Chrysologus, July 30, quoted in The Liturgy of the Hours for this day.

9. Robert E. McNally, S.J., *The Bible in the Early Middle Ages* (Atlanta: Scholars, 1986; reprint from 1959, Newman). McNally covers 650–1000 C.E. During these Dark Ages the manuscripts of the bible (mostly Vulgate) were worked on especially in the library in Northumbria, where Bede and Alcuin lived and had good resources. The illuminated manuscripts and the plastic art and stained glass windows attest to a creative spirit, but there was little of this in exegesis. The monks simply repeated the fathers for piety and morals.

10. The topic of normativity is a frequent concern of Protestant writers—for example, Paul Achtemeier, *The Inspiration of Scripture: Problems and Proposals* (Philadelphia: Westminster, 1980); James Barr, *Holy Scripture: Canon, Authority and Criticism* (Philadephia: Westminster, 1983); Harris R. Laird, *Inspiration and Canonicity of the Bible: Contemporary Evangelical Perspectives* (Grand Rapids: Zondervan, 1969); George W. Coats and Burke O. Long (eds.), *Canon and Authority* (Philadelphia: Fortress, 1977); C.H. Dodd,*The Authority of the Bible* (New York: Harper Bros., 1929); Garrett Green (ed.), *Scriptural Authority and Narrative Interpretation* (Philadelphia: Fortress, 1987); Paul Hanson, "Biblical Authority Reconsidered," *Horizons of Biblical Theology* 11 (1989), 57–79.

11. George Lindbeck commented in *Ratzinger Conference*, 89: "Even the Roman Catholic scriptural renewal anticipated as a result of the liturgical reforms of Vatican II and its emphasis on preaching and bible study seems moribund on the popular level. My experience is that the Roman Catholic undergraduates who take religion in the university at which I teach are now less scripturally literate than twenty odd years ago when they had been drilled on pre-Vatican II catechisms."

12. Robert Bruce Robinson, *Roman Catholic Exegesis Since Divino Afflante Spiritu* (SBL Dissertation Series, #111, Atlanta: Scholars, 1988).

13. Robert M. Grant and David Tracy, *A Short History of the Interpretation of the Bible* (Philadelphia: Fortress, 1984).

8

The Personal Resident Alien

Chapter 6 illustrated briefly how Paul reinterpreted the basic story of Jesus from his Jewish background and from the necessary myths of the race. Chapter 7 traced the history of how the community reshaped the tradition to meet varying needs and from varying competencies. Now it is time to consider how we too are personally subject to such Resident Aliens, good and bad, which, like an underwater current, push and pull our convictions in different directions.

1. Interpreters Are Diverse

Our diversity and individuality start before birth with genes and DNA chains. That is the physical fact. That determines how we look, what abilities and weaknesses we have physically, intellectually and emotionally, etc. Medical science now tries to modify what was wrong, but succeeds only to a very limited degree.

But then we must add in the specifics of a time and place on the planet. Hot or cold, benign or hostile, prosperous or starving—those facts of environment have an effect on the way we shall look at the physical world and the people around us.

They affect the kind of education we get. Education may be informal and traditional as in tribes in developing areas; it may be formal but very time-conditioned as in our world. The most important part of our education is what we learn at home. If we are taught well, we become connected with parents, grandparents, our extended family. We learn something of their history and much of their way of acting. The stories define our family character. Each of us is individually shaped, and yet it is within a tradition. We pick up attitudes toward one another, ways of cooperating, "doing the chores," being reckless or routine, bold or fearful, calm or excited and so on through a host of attitudinal responses. In various measures we accept or reject what is handed down to us.

We know much about our own societal problems of drugs, violence, abuse, irresponsibility, fadism, and gangs, and we tend to trace back so much of it to family life. Society, at least civilized society, seems to be losing its grip on discipline as the family loses importance. Yet despite disclaimers and proclamations of the death of marriage and the family, we still have the common sense to know that the family is the basic unit of society, and that when it goes, the whole of society is threatened. We are present but we are also past.

Our formal education is much more changeable. We do not learn from McGuffey's Reader; we learn on computers and from programmed courses. We are under the heavy influence of philosophical concepts of education which we may or may not advert to. We learn as citizens of the United States.

We learn a language. Thousands of them exist on the planet. But we learn our language. Some of us are bi-lingual or multi-lingual from childhood, yet we normally associate with one language as our own. We learn the signs and symbols of our culture, whether they are signs which animals leave or the traffic signs which we erect. We learn to respond to these instinctively as we learn to respond to the sound signs of our language. We become "street-wise" to many other subtle indicators about which others who do not belong to our tribe are ignorant.

2. Interpreters Seek Unity

And here we have one of those facts which does not yield to proclamations and protests and dire predictions. Without much logic we cling to the nesting need. Without a name and a home we are nothing—or at least lost. Those of uncertain parentage search for years to find their biological parents no matter how much love and security have been given them by others. We pity the "homeless" not simply because they are cold or exposed, but because they are lost. The same happens in religious allegiance.[1]

Psychiatrists and counselors deal with persons who have lost their way. Madness is not imbecility but logic without an anchor. The center around which we organize things has disappeared. We dream of "one world" or "the global village" or whatever our latest metaphor is, although we are aware that we have never been able to achieve much more than a limited amount of unity. Yet we want it. Even in religious ecumenism we admit that we need some single leader or Christianity has no effective central voice or symbol. We know instinctively that it simply will not work without some unity.

Out of all the disparate influences which have shaped our lives to the present moment, we fashion some sort of overview. Erik Erikson popularized the concept of the stages of growth. We begin as children and accept what the adults teach us. However, when we reach adolescence we normally begin to reject the overview which we inherited. We are more comfortable with conformity with our peers who are equally sloughing off their childhood. But we must finally grow out of this passing phase and we must fashion either raucously or gently our own view of what life is about and what are its priorities. If we do not, we emerge into adulthood without knowing who we are and where we are going.

Having achieved some sort of independence, most people then bind themselves back into the same interconnections of marriage and family. That, too, is a growing experience which makes us adjust our total view of life. It may or may not be a pleasant experience. A later crisis may force us to do the work of maturing out of due time. Those who become addicted to alcohol or drugs or work and survive often talk of their experience as a total reversal of values, a true conversion.

We emerge into mid-life and need to make more accommodations as children leave the home, achievement loses its savor, the milestones of success are passed without satisfaction. Life has become different once again and old age brings with it the realization that we are irrelevant, at least irrelevant to most of those around us. And where was the center of our life all along? What held us together, since we are survivors?

3. The Stages of Faith

James W. Fowler, building on Erik Erickson and Lawrence Kohlberg, has made clinical investigations into what he calls *Stages of Faith*.[2] All of these scholars are building on a theory called "structural-development"—namely, that there are certain structures of human development which seem to be universal whatever the culture and era. At the center of our being is some nucleus which seems to be ingrained. It is not a new idea. Philosophers and theologians before them have done the same, and contemporary psychologists, sociologists, etc., have endlessly disputed what it is. Plato thought that we were born with eternal ideas which simply were waiting to come into life. For him the ideas were more real than the thoughts which made us aware of them. Others said that we began with our minds as a blank tablet, but the writing which soon takes place follows definite patterns based on "universals."

Fowler introduced the insight that the changes which take place in us are not mere stages of change without any specific meaning. We grow toward something. From his contemporary clinical research he listed the most important contents as: (1) the centers of value, (2) the images of power, and (3) the master stories we tell ourselves. In a way we are back to the ancient rhetorical insight that it is the stories which are most important. Eventually the centers of value are expressed in images. We are also back to the mythological pictures, the "monomyth" of *The Hero with a Thousand Faces* of which Joseph Campbell was so intrigued. It is the golden grail or the *summa theologica* of the medieval theologians.

The images we use to express that idea are multiple, but the conviction remains that something definite is there at the center of our universe. Fowler pictures it as a spiral of ascending platforms where each stage grows out of the previous one (if we develop maturely) until we have found the final level which centers on the one thing necessary and accepts the doubts and ambiguities as irrelevant. With this we can live comfortably and give something of it to others. This is the generativity stage of Erikson's maturity. Full maturity makes us missionaries of a master idea which we can share with all the rest of our human family. Like Paul, we have a simple nucleus of facts around which we can satisfactorily organize what we need to know and make reasonable applications.

4. The Biblical Quest

If we go back to the Paul of 1 Thessalonians, we can see some of this emerging in him and in his hearers. At one point he talks of himself as a nursing mother (1 Thes 2:7). He appeals to their immature experience as Christians but looks forward to their continuing growth. Not all of them understood perfectly or accepted; a second letter was necessary. The commonalities of instinctive or learned myths, of a heritage of story-telling and of persuasive language gave him an initial entrance—what the formal rhetoricians call *inventio* or where to begin. He added his own personal vision, but he was aware that the truly persuasive force was from without—namely, the choice which God had made and followed up with gifts. These varied from person to person, as he says in the later letters.

Perhaps we can pause now and consider how this affects the scholarly enterprise. All of us, as scholars or as those listening to scholars, are at different stages of our maturity. We are arrested in our development at times, we regress, we destroy what we have already learned by our actions—and then we go forward. Those of us who are scholars become most immediately interested in the mechanics of our trade. We write papers and books, we lecture or discuss with younger students, we launch projects of our own on a hunch that we will find something. As professionals we are concerned that we are following the rules of the method which we have chosen for ourselves. Yet despite our diligence, we are sometimes dissatisfied with what we have done. Something is amiss and we cannot identify it. Needless to say, our readers, listeners, students, colleagues, etc., are often more dissatisfied than we are. However, we are so annealed to our professional methods and attitudes that we cannot take a larger look into ourselves and the recipients of our message to realize that our final criteria are not really all the professional methods which we assure ourselves and them that we are using.

Sometimes we forget the unconscious center or synthesis which we have been building up over the years. Our personal value system, our "center of values," to use Fowler's term, has been compounded of all those inherited and previously lived attitudes and conclusions which go into a human life. That is our true and deepest Resident Alien. Thomas Aquinas called it the understanding of all things under the aspect of eternity. Not bad.

When we interpret the sacred scriptures, all of this comes into play, whether we are professionals or lay persons. How much we shall understand depends far more on our stage of faith than on our stage of methodology. It carries conviction because of who we are. It appeals to others if we can establish contact with them on a similar level of faith. The sharing and the commitment are the most important elements for acceptance within the "classic hermeneutic" or *sensus fidelium*. We do not prove our conclusions; we simply state them because they are what we are and others out there respond because they have something of the same.

Jesus, in John's gospel, says: "No one can come to me unless the Father who sent me draw him" (Jn 6:44). It is frustrating. Neither wonders nor words nor logic can make disciples. Something happens from outside ourselves which makes us believers. So also the stories of conversion, whether to saintliness or simply to Alcoholics Anonymous or NarcAnon, etc., illustrate the commonality of that beginning. The "images of power" of which Fowler speaks must first collapse before we can recognize a higher power. That is what the myths are about; that is what recovery from any moral crisis is about. Then our master stories and the centers of value shift. So does our way of interpreting. The process is personal and individual. We reach out to the Hero with a Thousand Faces.

The bible has survived as a master book of spirituality because it captures these instinctive and universal needs.

Wherever we may be in the stages of growth, whatever our experience as individualized by birth, education, family, job may be, whatever may be our professional expertise, the bible gives us images which help us to universalize and organize that experience. The Catholic tradition speaks of an *analogia fidei*, an analogy of faith. This simply means that all of the tradition fits together in some way; it is a synthesis, not a disarrayed series of declarations. Vatican II spoke of the unity of the word of God, the bible, as somewhat similar to the Word of God, Jesus.[3] Each is a totality.

So also the church, as the body of Christ, is always in one of those stages of development. Paul speaks of the goal as "mature manhood, the full stature of Christ."[4] Yet in the final maturity it is one, individual and communal.

ENDNOTES

1. Andrew Greeley, *American Catholics Since the Council* (Chicago: Thomas More, 1985), 55–79, treats of this homing tendency of liberal Catholics and follows up with a later article on sociological surveys in "Why Catholics Stay in the Church" in *America* 157:3 (1987), 54–70: "They would remain regular churchgoers, but on their own terms, rejecting the official teaching but still showing up at church every week or nearly every week."

2. James W. Fowler, *Stages of Faith: The Psychology of Human Development and the Quest for Meaning* (San Francisco: Harper & Row, 1981). Fowler is a psychologist. The data in the book comes from interviews (cf. interview form in Appendix A) and from statistical analysis (Appendix B). His book is a summary of his work in research and teaching at Harvard Divinity School, Boston College and Emory University from 1972 to 1981. It was inspired by the work of Lawrence Kohlberg on structural-developmental research. Perhaps the shortest and clearest summary which Fowler gives of his structure of the Six Stages of Faith can be found on p. 290: STAGE 1—Infancy (Undifferentiated Faith)—mutuality, trust, and pre-images of the ground of being. STAGE 2—Early Childhood (Intuitive-Projective Faith)—rise of imagination, formation of images of numinous and an ultimate environment. STAGE 3—Childhood (Mythic-Literal

Faith)—the rise of narrative and the forming of stories of faith. STAGE 4—Adolescence (Synthetic-Conventional Faith)—The forming of identity and shaping of a personal faith. STAGE 5—Young Adulthood (Individuative-Reflective Faith)—reflective construction of ideology; formation of a vocational dream. STAGE 6—Adulthood (Conjunctive Faith)—paradox, depth and intergenerational responsibility for the world. Like Erikson this is basically developmental psychology derived from interviews. Our study has considered "adult" Christianity as normative. Paul in his use of the "tutor" image has recognized the developmental process. Numerous autobiographical references also indicate that "adult" Christian living was uneven for Paul personally—as he presumes that it was for others. Adult maturity is not an across-the-board phenomenon for anyone. Fowler is helpful in understanding this and in understanding the slow development of logical processes and then the abandonment of them (in some measure) in mature adulthood. He has also recognized the "identity" factor which accompanies social living. These are important points for our study.

3. Walter Abbott, *The Documents of Vatican II* (New York: America Press, 1966), Dogmatic Constitution on Divine Revelation, #13.

4. Ephesians 4:11–13 in the NAB reads: "And he gave some as apostles, others as prophets, others as evangelists, others as pastors and teachers, to equip the holy ones for the work of the ministry, for building up the body of Christ, until we all attain to the unity of faith, to mature manhood, to the extent of the full stature of Christ..." Paul uses the maturity metaphor often enough in his writings. Cf. 2 Corinthians 10:12–15 for an extended use in regard to himself and 1 Corinthians 3:1–2 as an admonition to the Corinthians to stop being children.

9

The Story Form of the Catholic Resident Alien

1. Our Presuppositions

A story is told of Thomas Aquinas that in his last illness he said that all he had written seemed to him as so much straw. Only the cross mattered. Not many people have read all that Thomas Aquinas wrote, and fewer still have a clear idea of what it means. But the point of the story is clear and satisfying. Many ordinary Christians have been encouraged to react like that in the face of death. This man was one of the greatest thinkers of our race, and yet at the end he could express his whole understanding and commitment in one word.

So what is it that makes a Catholic a Catholic? Or to use George Lindbeck's terms: What makes a "nuclear Christian"? And what has kept this faith alive for centuries? It is certainly not the proofs, the academic methods, the facts by themselves. Something is alive in "nuclear" Catholics which is compelling without rational proof.

Many methods of explaining the bible have been used by scholars and authorities in the course of the centuries; none of them has ever satisfied completely and finally. Each pacifies us for a while and then we become dissatisfied.[1] Society changes and what had met our needs no longer fits. How shall we find something which gives us at least some hope of going in the right direction? Shall we put our trust in the interpretation of the fathers? An ancient rule in Catholic theology says that when the fathers agree, we have a certain proof. But who knows when the fathers agree on anything beyond the basics? For centuries we made the *Summa*

Theologica of St. Thomas Aquinas the norm of proper teaching. But St. Thomas himself would have been aghast at considering his work as the *Summa Catholica*, the sum of all knowledge for Catholics. For a century or more, historical criticism has been accepted in most academic circles as *the* method. But our confidence in that is waning. The Ratzinger Conference at least identified that the real problem in interpretation lies beyond present specific methods.

Although there was no consensus at that conference, the participants were most taken by George Lindbeck's approach through the "classic hermeneutic." Translated into Catholic theological terms, that is *sensus fidelium*. But how does one find the "sense of the faithful" in today's world? Surely one does not take up a "scientific" poll of public opinion. Most such surveys are made by telephone. An operator asks for a personal identification of the person called such as Democrat, Republican, liberal, conservative, Catholic, Protestant, etc. Written questionnaires generally follow the same pattern. No check is made on how accurate the identification is. Andrew Greeley in his sociological survey of Catholics after Vatican II explained that he considered people he questioned as Catholics if they responded that they had been baptized as Catholics and had never formally renounced their religion.[2] That is the definition of the Code of Canon Law and it serves juridical purposes very well. But of course it says nothing about what kind of Catholic this person is or whether the person practices any religion. The results of such an opinion poll are certainly far from George Lindbeck's description: "The classic hermeneutic consists ultimately of what 'nuclear' Christians, to use Joseph Fichter's terminology, discover they believe at times of crisis and are willing to die for."[3]

But let me begin nearer to home. The gospel of John is the most popular course I teach to undergraduates. The reason is obvious on the first day of class. Most of the students want to hear more about how they are loved by Jesus. Popular psychology has already convinced them of that, and they have probably already identified with the Samaritan woman or Mary Magdalene, with Peter the shepherd or the beloved disciple as a loved one. Having reached these conclusions before beginning the study, they are shocked when I quote to them Alan Culpepper's observation that the gospel of John uses the word "love" more than any other gospel, but that Jesus is not portrayed as a very loving man.[4] They are also shocked to discover that the gospel is largely concerned about the sacrifices which the group of believers will be called upon to make as imitators of Jesus. Personalism and comforting feelings are not a large part of the message. Without knowing it, they already have a Resident Alien as an interpreter and they will insist on listening to that interpreter. I am not sure what they will accept in times of crisis.

Much of this book arose from my participation in a Continuing Task Force on Narrative Criticism at the Catholic Biblical Association. Most of the members also belong to the Society for Biblical Literature which is a much larger and denominationally uncommitted professional association. So I wonder what "Catholic" in the title of our association says about our presuppositions. Does it set us apart? Most of us are priests, religious or Catholic teachers of religion although we do have members from other denominations. They all have chosen to belong to and attend meetings of a professedly Catholic organization. There is something alien to our professional commitments which really brings us together. We too have a Resident Alien as interpreter. Of course, we do not all agree on what precisely that Resident Alien is or what it is saying.

Sometimes in scholarly journals we have an outburst of honesty which is refreshing. Sandra Schneiders has an article entitled: "The Samaritan Woman from a Feminist Ideology Viewpoint."[5] Evangelicals are apt to use "evangelical" in their titles, and Gabriel Fackre has written much and well about fundamentalism as an ideology and how this affects interpretation.[6]

Many of the great German scholars after World War I sought a pastoral approach. Prominent Lutherans, such as Dibelius, von Rad, Barth and Bultmann, all aimed at contemporary relevance. Bultmann proposed "demythologizing" the gospels.[7] He noted the similarity of the theme of the gospels to the stories of the "dying and rising gods" which were current in the Mediterranean world. As a first step, he wanted to understand how the gospels developed in order to embody this central myth. Having done so, he would then recast the story in contemporary images for understanding the dilemmas of modern life. It was not a bad idea. However, Bultmann got so involved in the mechanics of the process that he never got around to "remythologizing" the Christian theme. His followers often ignored "remythologizing" in their quest for academic orthodoxy. Catholics sometimes hid from it behind the sheltering presence of the Resident Alien of traditional orthodoxy.

The quest for "the method" or a normative principle has been going on for centuries. From the renaissance to the age of historical criticism (a very changing period) we passed through an era from commitment to sectarian conclusions about the bible which were fiercely defended to a reliance on facts as the only criterion of truth which was not imposed by outside authority. Objectivity was the proposed ideal, but it did not work out that way. It tended to become institutionalized subjectivity.

In medieval times the master idea which made universities possible was the conviction that we could put together a synthesis of all knowledge. The great *summas* of medieval times were organized around theology as the queen of the sciences, but every other bit of human knowledge had a pigeonhole somewhere. It was a truly universal and noble ideal even though we joke about the final author who wrote *De omnibus rebus et aliquibus aliis*, namely, "Concerning all things and some others." It was never completed.

Before that, in a very general way, the fathers of the church tried to unify their religious beliefs around concepts from Greek philosophy, particularly but not exclusively from Plato. The great doctrinal decisions of the fourth and fifth centuries were always expressed in philosophical terms. The end result, as often as not, was not logic but paradox. All the great distinctive truths of Christianity are paradoxes.

One could easily enough trace this back into the gospels and the other New Testament writings themselves. As scholars we are continuously beguiled by the desire to write a theology of the

New Testament. To do so we must have an organizing point. We have tried them all by this time—love, freedom, law, social service, the end time, the pilgrim people, etc. Popular preaching often follows the latest fads in biblical theology. Then biblical theology shows a tendency to self-destruct until a generation or so later it is revived as indispensable.[8] Despite our cleverness with methods, we do not usually unmask the Resident Alien and make it a house guest.

2. *The Story Approach to the Resident Alien*

Scholars down through the ages have given us very valuable insights into the meaning of the bible. However, they have not created faith nor defined its meaning. That has been left to the people.

The Catholic theological method has been the *sensus fidelium*, the understanding of the faithful. As noted previously, this is what Vatican II reasserted with clarity.

> The holy People of God shares also in Christ's prophetic office. It spreads abroad a living witness to Him, especially by means of a life of faith and charity and by offering to God a sacrifice of praise, the tribute of lips which give honor to His name (cf. Heb 13:15). The body of the faithful as a whole, anointed as they are by the Holy One (cf. Jn 2:20, 27), cannot err in matters of belief. Thanks to a supernatural sense of the faith which characterizes the People as a whole, it manifests this unerring quality when, "from the bishops down to the last member of the laity," it shows universal agreement in matters of faith and morals.[9]

So we are back to the age-old problem of how to define precisely how one knows the *sensus fidelium*. Something resides in the faithful (or "the church" if one avoids a separation between the laity and the hierarchy) which is alien to formal academic investigation or proof. When we make a statement of Catholic belief, we most often use the official decrees of church leaders,

such as councils, papal encyclicals, etc. A mere listing of proposi-
tions does not have great dramatic impact on people's lives.
Sometimes a statement of Catholic belief is bolstered, both by
historical studies and the *senus fidelium*. Our great creeds speak
the language of theological truth, of course, but they also speak
eloquently to people's hearts. What became the doctrine of the
Assumption of Mary first depended on the devotion and beliefs
of men and women throughout every age in the church. Yet it is
not entirely clear how the sense of the faithful is translated into
doctrinal theological statements. Indeed, the Tradition with a big
"T" can become confused at a certain point with the traditions
with a small "t," that is to say, customs.

3. The Jesus Story Today

Let me try a different approach to "the classic hermeneutic"
or *sensus fidelium*. Vatican II in its Constitution on Divine
Revelation repeated the ancient formula about the inspiration of
the bible by the Holy Spirit, but added the final note that
Scripture teaches "firmly, faithfully, and without error that truth
which God wanted put into the sacred writings for the sake of
our salvation."[11] It is "that truth...for the sake of our salvation"
which is important. The important things must be highlighted
first. Within the Christian tradition (as also within the Jewish
and Muslim ones) there is no doubt that the people interpret that
there is only one God. In the Christian tradition the people also
accept that Jesus Christ is divine as well as human, that the Son is
joined with a Father and a Spirit in a triune deity. We may continue this listing of a creed of faith to include all the basic beliefs.
Indeed it is the purpose of the Apostles' Creed and the Nicene
Creed, as they are called, to express the greatest commonality of
Christian belief.

But why do we accept this as the faith of the people? The individuals probably do not believe or understand every word of it,
at least in the full sense. However, the Jesus story enables us to
keep clear the basic story-line; this unites us at two levels: shared
belief and a way of living that arises from it.

4. The Jesus Story Among Catholics Today

I use Roman Catholics as a model of tradition here since I am more familiar with how my own people act; other Christian faiths need to assess what the story means in their own tradition. As Roman Catholics we need to look around to see what we really have in our common lived faith. Identifying a real Catholic, a "nuclear Christian," is fairly simple. First of all, the real Catholics go to Mass on Sundays. That may seem inconsequential and commonplace since people of many other denominations also go to church. However, Catholics are going for a distinctive reason. They are going to join in the re-presentation of the death and resurrection of Jesus made visible in the sacrifice. Catholics will also listen to the Jesus story in the readings and the homily, preached by someone commissioned by the people of God through appointed officials. The community is formally recalling and repeating the Jesus story. And we keep coming back.

Moreover, in churches throughout the world some Catholics consistently keep coming to mass on weekdays. They don't need to do so and there is not ordinarily much splendor to satisfy the senses at these weekday celebrations. Yet they will not be driven away from participating in the "word and sacrament." Whether many or a few, they will be in church, and when a priest is not available, they will be saddened. In the history of the church and at the present time there may be penalties for them to do so. It may be no more than the social disapproval of family and friends, or some work-related restriction which demands a sacrifice. But for them that is what the mass is all about. In times of persecution the penalty may be loss of goods and position; it has often enough meant death. But the story must go on in the lived actions of the faithful Catholics.

The liturgy is the most powerful way in which the Jesus story is kept alive today, "the summit toward which the activity of the Church is directed; at the same time it is the fountain from which all her power flows," as Vatican II said.[12] It is the people who have made the liturgy necessary as a dramatic way of stating the basic truths of the need for salvation, the coming of a Savior

INTERPRETING THE BIBLE

physically among us, the forgiveness of our sins and the hope of heaven. Whatever else may flow from theology will need to take its place below this. Even Vatican Council II invoked such a principle of "hierarchy of truths" in its Decree on Ecumenism.[13]

The liturgical year conforms to the basic beliefs of the people. In the hope of salvation it begins with Advent, a time of waiting through the dying season. Christmas hails the coming of the newborn Savior. Epiphany reminds us of our mission to the world. Lent is the sad and honest time of penance. The last days of Lent celebrate our liberation in the death, burial and resurrection of the savior, to use Paul's brief summary. Pentecost empowers us to live the Christian life to the full during the "ordinary time" of the rest of the year. In our normal path toward maturity these feasts and seasons correspond to our own developing needs. The people know the basic truths as they live their lives. No scholar needs to explain "eschatology" to them; they know where life is going.

The adornment of the liturgy with vestments, sacred vessels, art and music has also been an instinctive urge of the people to express their belief in the basic truths. When something needs to be done to beautify the church, some donor always seems to come forward. Often in trying times the church has provided almost the only beauty, however meager, in the lives of the poor. Their understanding of a good and beautiful God needs no academic definition. They seek the expression of it which is already present and they will gladly offer their ministry to provide for it.

The people do not need to be told to praise God. Surely the scholars can point out the endless praises of God in the biblical stories, even in the difficult ones. One might note that the book of Psalms is called in Hebrew the *Sefer tahillim*, the book of praises, and in Latin the morning prayer is called "Lauds" or praises. The faithful do not need to be instructed that this is the center of our relationship to God. They may need to be reminded, but they already believe it. It is the liturgy which tells that story.

Perhaps the cult of saints can serve as an illuminating example. A recent book has pointed out how uniquely democratic or popular the canonization of saints actually is.[14] The designating of some people as saints begins with popular acclaim, not with hierarchical decree. The people discern in some individuals attitudes and actions which say that this life is a model of what we really believe. The idea of "saint" usually starts with ethics. Martyrs die for their faith while praying for their executioners. A Francis of Assisi launches a whole movement of mystical poverty which has immense popular appeal. A Vincent de Paul devises humble means for ordinary people to help vast numbers of the poor, the homeless and the sick. These values endure. Today we and others hold up Mother Teresa of Calcutta as an exemplar of Christian charity. The people are defining what a Catholic is by actual living. The ethical dimension gets clarified first in real people.

What I have said about the role of the people in no way derogates from the authority of the pope and the bishops. Someone must say the final word as to what the people believe. That was expressly stated in the last defined dogma, that of the Assumption of Mary. The pope consulted the bishops as to the devotions and beliefs of the faithful in their dioceses. It is the people who have the instinct to take the initiative; the hierarchy places the stamp of approval on it.

5. The Story Among the Professionals

The professional interpreters have a different problem. The complexities of sophisticated methods do not bother them. They understand that the difficult languages have common patterns of communication, as the structuralists have researched. Beyond the endless details of archeological discoveries are common patterns of development. Beyond the intricacies of rhetoric such as deconstructionism or reader-response are common ways in which we go about our understanding of one another. These can easily confuse the ordinary reader but are the common business of the scholars.

The problem of the professionals is to put first things first, to establish a hierarchy of truths which is necessary for salvation or a spiritual view of life. That aspect in particular often has little practical value either in commercial writing or in academic status. Reader-response to their own writing can end with a calculation of how many books will be sold, not with how well the readers will live a Christian life.

Literary critics are familiar with "reader-response." In their research this often means the response of the original readers of the manuscript. Great effort is, therefore, expended to discover the historical and social circumstance of the original readers. The present readers who are quite different historically, socially and personally often get ignored. If the book doesn't sell, obviously there has been no reader-response and it may leave the author quite confused. The failure may not have been in the quality of the research or the felicity of expression, but in the lack of interpretation of the readers. The writer did not speak to their living conditions. My emphasis on the primacy of the "nuclear Christians" is an appeal to scholars or writers like myself to have the humility to look around at the world we live in and learn from common people the things they believe and need for good, solid living.

6. The Crisis of the Historical Jesus

On one crucial point we know that this Christian mythology departs from the standard pattern. Myth takes place in the uncharted land of timelessness. It is simply an attempt to explain in story what we all experience and hope for. The Jesus story, however, takes place in time. It has an historical basis.

The great problem about the historical Jesus is not whether he was historical or whether every detail related in the New Testament is factually true. The great problem is to discern how much of an historical nucleus is required to validate the interpretation which grew out of it. Oddly, the most recent renewal of the "quest for the historical Jesus" has come from two Catholics.[15] Both, of course, support an historical Jesus of some sort but do not come to grips with what seems to be the crucial problem. Once again literary criticism should be of some help. How much of any story needs to be true before people will accept it? That depends on how willing we are to accept that truth emerges in different ways. It is difficult to make a good story out of straightforward scientific fact. Some science fiction is so loaded with technical details that we cannot assimilate it into our common experience.[16] Some psychological stories or movies are so centered on inward human reactions that we cannot follow the plot. Some plots are so predictable that we cannot accept them as real. Real life is so full of unanswered questions, absurdities, personality quirks, ironies and paradoxes that we appreciate the art of a story-teller who can persuade us that a pattern does exist in all this, even if it is a mysterious pattern made elsewhere. In fact, mystery is in many ways the most satisfying real experience of our lives, for it stretches out limitlessly. The measure of truth in a good story is not immediately how factual it is but how truly it conforms to our own experiences. This is what literary criticism should do.

The experience of self-help groups who use a Twelve-Step program is perhaps illustrative. There are popular speakers who specialize in the "before-and-after" plot. It quickly pales in the hard living of the program. That kind of story has probably been related so often that it has become stale and lacks the impact of reality. New members are cherished since their remembrance of the need for salvation is still vivid and unmanipulated. The interpretation which triggers change depends upon the real experience that some power higher than themselves saved them when they were helpless. Without the reality of the experience, however, the interpretation which follows is hollow and simply bookish. The story must be based on fact and the interpretation must come out of it.

Literary criticism is largely a matter of telling a story. The story does demand facts to trigger it. How many facts? To be convincing, that depends on the real reader. If one makes a preliminary pre-judgment that only scientific and objective facts are real experience, then the field for interpretation is severely limited. Academic biblical interpretation can easily become sterile from being constrained within such limits which are only a small part of human experience. Before we can accept that there was an historical Jesus and that he was a savior, one must have had some personal experience of it. The experience may come from listening to Christian preaching or from some personal crisis in life or from some mysterious experience. However it comes about, it is needed to get a clear insight into the whole. Paul began with that kind of personal experience and found that the "was crucified, was buried, was raised" was enough historical fact to trigger an insight into how he should live.

Most of us who write or lecture on biblical subjects do not write children's books. It is too difficult. We leave that to parents. We realize that children have a limited area of experience but great imagination. At the other extreme, few of us these days write "apologetics," that is, books intended to prove to unbelievers that we are right. The reasons for being an unbeliever are myriad, and until we know the personal story of this individual, we are talking to the wind. We need some commonality of real experience before we can begin. Literary criticism can aid the quest for the historical Jesus by looking at the conclusions which the believers have already accepted. They did not accept them on logic or proof; they accepted them on need. The need was real. The Jesus of faith undoubtedly dominates the New Testament writings. But the faith relied on a real experience. Paul makes a capital point of that. "If Christ has not been raised, then empty [too] is our preaching; empty, too, your faith" (1 Cor 15:14). But unless the hearers have also had a real experience of death and resurrection, our faith is also in vain.

It is literary criticism far more than historical criticism which can bring the two together. We need honest inquiry into the problem of the historical Jesus, but this alone will not solve the problem. The tomb is empty and will remain empty without the people of the Resurrection living the final events of the story. We must understand the art of narrative in our own lives.

ENDNOTES

1. Interest in the subject is high, especially among Protestants, as the following random listing of entries indicates: Carl Braaten, *The Whole Counsel of God* (Philadelphia: Fortress, 1974); Albert Sundberg, Jr., "The Bible Canon and the Christian Doctrine of Interpretation," *Interpretation* 29 (1975), 352–371; Paul Achtemeier, *The Inspiration of*

Scripture: Problems and Proposals (Philadelphia: Westminster, 1980); James Barr, *Holy Scripture: Canon, Authority and Criticism* (Philadelphia: Westminster, 1983); Thomas Hoffman, "Inspiration, Normativeness, Canonicity and the Unique Sacred Character of the Bible," *Catholic Biblical Quarterly* 44 (1982), 447–469; George W. Coats and Burke O. Long (eds.), *Canon and Authority* (Philadelphia: Fortress, 1977); Charles E. Winquist, *Practical Hermeneutics: A Revised Agenda for the Ministry* (Missoula: Scholars Press, 1980); Hans Küng and Jurgen Moltmann (eds.), *Conflicting Ways of Interpreting the Bible* (New York: Seabury, 1980); Paul Ricoeur, *Essays on Biblical Interpretation* (Philadelphia: Fortress, 1980); Frederick Greenspahn (ed.), *Scripture in the Jewish and Christian Traditions: Authority, Interpretation and Relevance* (Nashville: Abingdon, 1980); Richard John Neuhaus (ed.), *Biblical Interpretation in Crisis: The Ratzinger Conference on Bible and Church* (Grand Rapids: Eerdmans, 1989); Garrett Green (ed.), *Scriptural Authority and Narrative Interpretation* (Philadelphia: Fortress, 1987); Stephen D. Moore, *The Literary Theoretical Criticism Challenge and the Gospels* (New Haven: Yale University Press, 1989).

2. Andrew Greeley, *The Catholic Myth* (New York: Scribners, 1990), 108.

3. George Lindbeck, "Scripture, Consensus and Community," *This World*, 23 (1988), 5. This is also found in *The Ratzinger Conference*.

4. R. Alan Culpepper, *Anatomy of the Fourth Gospel* (Philadelphia: Fortress, 1983), 111. Culpepper is acutely right.

5. Sandra Schneiders, "Feminist Ideology Criticism and Biblical Hermeneutics," *Biblical Theology Bulletin* 17 (1989), 3–19.

6. Gabriel J. Fackre has written much in an eminently fair way about fundamentalism, e.g., *The Religious Right and Christian Faith* (Grand Rapids: Eerdmans, 1982); "Evangelical Hermeneutics: Commonality and Diversity," *Interpretation* 43 (1989), 117–123 and this within the larger context of his extensive work on systematics: *The Christian Story: Authority: Scripture in the Church for the World* (Grand Rapids: Eerdmans, Vol. 1, 1983; Vol. 2, 1987). Historical critics often betray their presuppositions by the titles they give their work, especially those concerning the historical Jesus. It would be helpful if more of us did so.

7. Rudolf Bultmann, *New Testament and Mythology*, Schubert M. Ogden, ed. (Philadelphia: Fortress, 1984).

8. Kristar Stendahl's article "Biblical Theology" in George A. Buttrick (ed.) *Interpreter's Dictionary of the Bible*, 418–432, is often cited as the classic resume of biblical theology. James Barr has remarked that new attempts at organizing biblical theology around a central theme gen-

erally have a life of about twenty years before the program is abandoned. Then the need for a synthesis around some theme which is really outside the text reasserts itself and the quest begins anew. Cf. James Barr, *The Bible in the Modern World* (New York: Harper & Row, 1973).

9. Walter Abbott, S.J., *The Documents of Vatican II* (New York: America Press, 1966), 29, Dogmatic Constitution on the Church. The first schema of the tract from a juridic viewpoint (cf. Acta I, 1, 18–19) had a section on who were members. The second schema of September 30, 1962 dropped the *ecclesia militans*, "the church battling," and called this section *De Ecclesia in terris peregrinante*, "the church pilgrimaging on earth" (Acta II, 1, 219), but it was still juridic and said nothing about "without error," which under some circumstances was reserved for the pope and councils. The third revision (Acta II, 4, 18) did mention the whole church as infallible, but the title still was the members of the church in a juridic sense, not in a prophetic role. Archbishop Ritter of St. Louis then (December 1, 1962) intervened to protest that it was the whole church which under some circumstances was infallible. His English text can be found in Vincent Yzermans, *American Participation in the Second Vatican Council* (New York: Sheed and Ward, 1967), 48; the Latin text is in Acta I, 4, 137. Session II began with what is the present outline. Session 80 in Acta III, 1, 185 has the first expression about the whole people of God being anointed with the Spirit and being without error. This was accepted, and after four votes were taken on Chapter 2, the whole document was approved. At any rate, it seems to have been Ritter (and probably Nicholas Persich, C.M. who was his *peritus*) who triggered the whole thing.

10. Judge John F. Noonan, Jr. of the United States Court of Appeals has tried to trace his own academic and legal career in "A Backward Look" (*Religious Studies Review*, 18 [1992], 111–112) through his earlier historical investigations of such ethical issues as usury, contraception, abortion and marriage. He finds that he was always looking for how the people affecting and affected by such situations actually responded. There was flexibility in the tradition as it was applied, but there was always a firm basis of moral values which stayed the same.

11. Abbott, *The Documents of Vatican II*, Dogmatic Constitution on Divine Revelation, #11.

12. Abbott, *The Documents of Vatican II*, Constitution on the Sacred Liturgy, #10.

13. Abbott, *The Documents of Vatican II*, Decree on Ecumenism, #11:

"When comparing doctrines, they (Catholic ecumenicists) should remember that in Catholic teaching there exists an order or 'hierarchy' of truths, since they vary in their relationship to the foundation of the Christian faith."

14. Kenneth Woodward, *Making Saints* (New York: Simon and Schuster, 1990).

15. As noted before, the problem began in its acute form with Albert Schweitzer's book, *The Historical Jesus*. Oddly enough the last two major books on the subject have been written by Catholic authors: John Meier, *A Marginal Jew: Rethinking the Historical Jesus* (New York: Doubleday, 1991), Vol. 1, and by John Dominic Crossan, *The Historical Jesus, The Life of a Mediterranean Jewish Peasant* (San Francisco: Harper, 1991).

16. Carl Sagan, *Contact* (New York: Simon and Schuster Pocket Books, 1985). Sagan is a distinguished astronomer who has written science fiction and lectured widely. This story concerns contact with a galaxy which is sending a message that needs decoding. The technical explanations are awesome, and one eventually gets tired of the name-dropping. The climax comes when five scientists are transported to this galaxy and are reunited with dead loved ones. The novel has a fundamentalist preacher who is representative of what Sagan thinks religion is about. The preacher fares badly. The climax, however, is right out of the mythology of ancestor worship, although Sagan doesn't seem to place much emphasis on the mythological origin.

10

Conclusion

The originating question was: Why do people interpret the bible in such different ways? The investigation tried to reveal, sometimes in wandering ways, that the commonalities which make any interpretation possible are largely the Resident Aliens—namely:

Story-telling techniques.

Mythologies, even unperceived.

Language structures which allow communication.

Ritual as story-telling.

Groups will unite, establish and identify and separate themselves from others because of the Resident Aliens. People will cling to that identity beyond logic or data and beyond every attempt to dissuade them by any means, even death. Within the Christian tradition this is the "classic hermeneutic" or the "sense of the faithful." It is simple, direct and practical.

On the other hand, there is always a "local habitation and a place" for the images and the interpretations. Zion always was the place for the dwelling of Yahweh; the eucharist is the dwelling place of the Lord Jesus for Catholics. Such places are sacred and separate. But they are always individual. The images of the savior-hero are always tied to local needs of the times and expressed in the contemporary idiom. The quest goes on because the crises of personal maturing and social disaster are always different and changing in specific ways. Yet at the end we always discover the need for a savior from without. The monomyth of *The Hero with a Thousand Faces* always wins.

Within the Catholic tradition the basic identity has a particularly strong root because the tradition of the faithful as teacher is so enduring and yet so flexible. Liturgy has been extremely adaptable to local needs and yet it remains ecumenical within the identifiable Catholic Church. Story-telling both about the Jesus event and about the heroes of Christian virtue has prevailed in visible but distinctive ways.

This book has been based on a literary approach to the biblical data. That seems to offer potential for further understanding of the basic plots which convey the sense of the faithful. It also offers an horrendous area for distortion if it is not always closely tied to the basics. This book has also been an attempt to understand with some reasonableness what the sense of the faithful is. However, why men and women should become and remain "the faithful" always escapes into mystery. "No one can come to me unless the Father who sent me draw him..." (Jn 6:44).